CW00449342

Mid ~uiiuik Light Railway

by
Nicholas Comfort

THE OAKWOOD PRESS

© Oakwood Press and Nicholas Comfort 1997

British Library Cataloguing in Publication Data
A Record for this book is available from the British Library
ISBN 0 85361 509 8

First published 1964, reprinted 1972 and 1977
Second edition 1986
Third edition 1997

Typeset by Oakwood Graphics.
Repro by Ford Graphics, Ringwood, Hants.
Printed by Alpha Print (Oxford) Ltd, Witney, Oxon.

Brockford and Wetheringsett station (note 'Brockford' nameboard) as a train from Laxfield arrives. The building to the right has survived to adorn the reconstructed station, that on the left also served as a telephone kiosk. *Lens of Sutton*

Title Page: A rare photograph of the first locomotive on the 'Middy' - Manning, Wardle 'K' class 0-6-0 tank No. 1134 with contractor's wagon and workers, on what appears from its unevenness to be Jackson's original track. Note the heap of just-cleared foliage.
P. Rose

By the same author:
The Lost City of Dunwich, Terence Dalton, 1994.
Brewer's Politics - A Phrase and Fable Dictionary, Cassell, 2nd Edition 1995.
The Tunnel: The Channel and Beyond (Co-author), Ellis Horwood, 1987.

Published by
The Oakwood Press
P.O. Box 122, Headington, Oxford OX3 8LU

Contents

No. 65447 comes to rest on the level crossing at Laxfield station with the 11.15 am from Haughley, 1st September, 1951. Traffic on the 'B' road to Stradbroke had to wait until the engine had backed the train away from the platform and run-round.   *H.C. Casserley*

Ex-GER 'J15' class 0-6-0 No. 65471, still in its LNER livery, arrives at Stradbroke from Haughley in 1948.   *Dr Ian C. Allen*

The re-created Brockford station in May 1995, showing the Mendlesham station building on the platform created from the old cattle dock. The hut in the foreground was originally the station building at Wilby; the original Brockford platform stood behind it. Hudswell, Clarke 0-6-0 No. 1604 is in the platform road with GER coach No. 1266 and two of the line's collection of wagons.
                                                                                                                                David Chappell

Introduction

When I first set out over 30 years ago to chronicle the history of the Mid-Suffolk Light Railway - the 'Middy' to those who knew it - the story seemed firmly set in the past. More than a decade had elapsed since the line's closure and its route and buildings were disappearing as local agriculture prospered, so the task at hand was to record the life and death of a line conceived in over-enthusiasm and never completed, which survived as a picturesque rural byway for almost half a century before yielding to the inevitable. When I expanded my text in 1986 to give a fuller account of the line's promotion, operation and closure, I was looking at a fuzzier picture; traces of the line were harder to find, and the years had thinned the ranks of those who remembered it. With this third edition, however, the story has a present tense once more and, with luck, a future. For since 1990 a determined band of volunteers has been working to reconstruct a section, at least, of the line, and while we may never again see trains cover the 19 miles from Haughley Junction to Laxfield, a steam service over a portion at Brockford and maybe even over the 2½ miles from there to Aspall does look capable of achievement - sadly without any of the locomotives or rolling stock of the original line, though several station buildings have survived. As this edition went to press, the reconstituted MSLR Company was in consultations with the local authority after an initial refusal of planning permission for a working line, but hopes were high that an accommodation could be reached. This further expanded celebration of the Mid-Suffolk Light Railway traces the way an improbable dream has started to become reality, but also tells the original story in more detail and with, I believe, greater accuracy.

That story is one of a railway that ran out of steam, yet survived to serve one of the remotest parts of East Anglia for two generations. The Mid-Suffolk was conceived at the turn of the century as a network of standard gauge lines conveying farm produce and passengers from an area previously unserved and without major centres of population to no fewer than four junctions with Great Eastern main lines. What it became was vastly different: a line from Haughley, junction of the GER lines from Ipswich to Norwich and Bury St Edmunds, to the picturesque and remote village of Laxfield, and two short sections salvaged from uncompleted portions of the line which for a few years carried freight alone. This lowering of expectations, which carried within it the seeds of failure, was the result of financial and routing problems once work had begun, the ruin of one of the line's chief backers and disputes with the contractors. It took Herculean efforts by management and staff to get the line cleared by the Board of Trade to operate a passenger service at all, and when the Grouping came in 1923 the London and North Eastern Railway did its level best to avoid taking responsibility for the undertaking, later proposing to replace it with a road. From then until the early days of Nationalisation the Mid-Suffolk pursued an unspectacular though at times entertaining existence, becoming a local institution even for the ever-increasing numbers who never used it, and known to enthusiasts as a line with primeval stock, arcane working practices and a high attrition rate among its innumerable level crossing gates.

By contrast with the Colonel Stephens' lines, the Mid-Suffolk after its absorption in the LNER lacked the make-do-and-mend romance and the precarious existence which attracted railway writers and photographers, and but for the fortuitous presence as a local GP of Dr Ian C. Allen, noted in both fields, it would have been almost unchronicled. Anyone writing about the line owes a considerable debt to Dr Allen, not only for his photographic and anecdotal record but for the effect of his work on others who came to see for themselves from the late 1940s, once it was clear that closure was only a matter of time. At the very end it also inspired John Hadfield's *Love On A Branch Line*, which while published in 1959 only received the popularity it deserved when serialised by the BBC 35 years later. I am grateful to Mr Hadfield and the Alastair Press for permission to quote from it.

Authors given the chance to produce an expanded edition often maintain that, in view of the errors and inadequacies they have been able to remedy, they wish the previous editions had never appeared. I cannot say that, not so much because what first appeared from the Oakwood Press in 1963, or even in 1986, was anything like the last word, but because much information in this present account was contributed by readers who felt more might be said. In particular I owe thanks to the late Canon E.W. Blyth and Mr Michael Windeatt, Mr R. Trudgett, Mr David Butterworth, Mr P.C. Dorrington, Mrs Jill Renvoize, and Mr M.C. Richards. I must also acknowledge the extent to which I have drawn on material in Peter Paye's comprehensive book on the Mid-Suffolk Light Railway, published at much the same time as my own previous edition, to remedy errors or omissions; this book, however, continues to have a very different thrust from Mr Paye's. Special thanks are due to the officers of the Mid-Suffolk Light Railway Society, especially David Chappell, Paul Davey and John Brodribb, who have helped me piece together the story of how the preservation scheme came about. My thanks for permission to publish original plans go to the County Archivist, Suffolk Record Office (Ipswich branch), whose staff have been consistently helpful as were those of its East Suffolk predecessor, the Public Record Office and the archivists of the erstwhile British Transport Commission. The librarian of the *East Anglian Daily Times* gave valuable help, and I am grateful to that newspaper for permission to quote from it at length. Mr R.W. Kidner, proprietor of the Oakwood Press when the first edition appeared and until 1984, delved deep to unearth details of the financial ruin of the Mid-Suffolk's first Chairman, Mr F.S. Stevenson, without which the original work would have been an even paler shadow than it was. To his successor, Mrs Jane Kennedy, I owe both the chance to make improvements not just once but twice, and the impetus to carry the project through.

Finally I owe an incalculable debt to my wife, Corinne Reed Comfort, for enabling me to produce my third and longest manuscript at a time when domestic and work pressures have made it harder than ever to carve out the time for such a project.

Nicholas Comfort,
Swalcliffe,
Oxon,
February 1997.

Chapter One

Promotion of the Line
and Early Tribulations

Few parts of rural England have changed so little over the centuries as central East Suffolk. While its fortunes have fluctuated, its staple has always been agriculture: cattle, more recently grain, and root crops. It contains no significant centres of population and has never been threatened with urban development. The industrial revolution passed it by, save for the application of steam and later diesel power to the day-to-day tasks of farming. Its fields may have grown larger, but its landscape, gently undulating with moated farms and increasingly hilly country toward Ipswich and the coast, would offer few surprises to an inhabitant from the past. The villages, too, would be easily recognisable, dominated by fine church towers and with inns, timber-framed houses and such delights as Laxfield's brick-and-timber Guildhall (also housing a bank) having survived the centuries. Equally the charm of Debenham's hilly snugness has survived a catastrophic fire in the 18th century. The population has fluctuated, with the drift from the land in the late 19th century and a middle-class influx in recent years as East Anglia's closeness to the Continent brought prosperity and more people worked by computer from home. But the place has kept its spirit: in Laxfield where the shoemaker William Noyes was burned at the stake in 1557 for his Protestant convictions, villagers still refer to Anglicans and Baptists as 'the two religions'.

Lacking towns or industry, it was not surprising that this sizeable area some 25 miles square escaped the 'railway mania' of the early and mid-Victorian era, save for two short branches to Framlingham and Eye. Railways were primarily built to link centres of population, and where Suffolk was concerned this meant the promotion of lines from Ipswich to London, Bury St Edmunds, Norwich and the chain of towns just inland from the coast *en route* for Lowestoft and Great Yarmouth, with branches to the most deserving communities which had been missed out. First proposals for a line from Ipswich to Norwich as early as 1826 did involve a route slicing through this area, the southern portion approximating to the Mid-Suffolk Light Railway's (MSLR) intended route between Westerfield and Debenham. Yet the first line actually built, in 1846, ran from Ipswich to Bury; the route to Norwich diverging from it at Haughley followed in 1848/49, the Halesworth-Haddiscoe section of the East Suffolk line in 1854, and the Tivetshall-Harleston line which began boxing off the area from the north along the Waveney Valley in 1856. The 1st June, 1859 brought the opening of the Ipswich-Halesworth and Haddiscoe-Yarmouth lines to complete a through route, together with the Framlingham and Snape branches and the sections from Saxmundham to Leiston and Beccles to Lowestoft. These were followed by Leiston-Aldeburgh in 1860, Harleston-Beccles between 1860 and 1863, and the Eye branch in 1867. From 1862 all these lines came under the umbrella of the Great Eastern Railway (GER).

A railway to fill the gap between these of lines was now conspicuous by its absence, but the Great Eastern, with its monopoly position and tight finances,

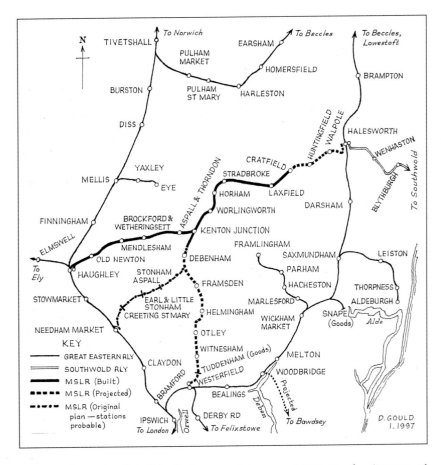

A map of the Mid-Suffolk Light Railways as first proposed: 1898/9. The alignment of each of the lines planned was to undergo a number of changes, save for that to Needham Market which was abandoned very early. In particular the 'kink' north of Otley was straightened out. The Old Newton station was on the site of the short-lived Brown Street siding, not the more durable Gipping goods station a little to the east, Wilby station has yet to be thought of. The southern approach route to Halesworth can be clearly seen.

was now fully stretched and in no mood for speculative schemes. Moreover recession had set in on the land after the golden era which culminated in the 1850s, and the rural population, which had been comparatively dense, was fast ebbing away, the 'black year' of 1879 seeing the trend at its height. The population of the stately village of Stradbroke, not then served by rail, peaked at 1,800 in the middle of the century and by 1891 was down to 1,069, falling more slowly thereafter; the decline of smaller communities was as marked.

Economic decline, coupled with the difficulties which farmers well away from the Great Eastern's through routes experienced in getting their livestock and produce to market, led to pressure in those areas as yet unserved by rail for the gap to be filled . . . if not by the 'main line' company, then by somebody else. An abortive attempt to start an independent company was made in 1889, but what finally prompted a definite scheme, here as in other parts of the country where a railway to anything like main line standards was not feasible, was the passage in 1896 of the Light Railways Act. This encouraged the promotion of minor lines by setting less taxing signalling and safety standards in return for a 25 mph speed limit, and by enabling schemes to be approved by the President of the Board of Trade on the advice of the Light Railway Commissioners, instead of through the cumbersome procedure of a Parliamentary Bill. Passage of the Act had the effect intended, a large number of schemes of varying soundness being promoted up and down the country, many of them ready planned to take advantage of the lower costs the new legislation would permit. While a fair proportion of railways envisaged once the Act was on the statute book never got beyond the drawing board, the Mid-Suffolk Light Railway was one that did.

The initiative for the line came from Mr H.L. Godden, of Jeyes and Godden, a London firm of civil engineers, who worked up detailed plans, then wrote to parish councils and landowners in October 1898 suggesting that if some funds could be raised locally, he could find other backers. Mr Godden met such a response that on 1st February, 1899 he was able to lead a deputation to the Board of Trade to discuss the project. Interested parties met at Debenham later that month, and other meetings followed to form local committees along the proposed route of the line. Mr Bernard Kilby of Staines, who had worked with Mr Godden on light railway schemes for Grimsby and the Trent Valley, offered to raise half the preliminary expenses and at a meeting in Ipswich the project was formally launched. Lord Rendlesham, Chairman of Suffolk County Council, began in the chair, but made way for Mr Francis Stevenson of Playford Mount, near Woodbridge, who was elected Chairman of the new company. Mr Stevenson had since 1885 been Liberal MP for the Eye division, covering most of the area to be served; his involvement with the scheme was to be long, intimate and ultimately ruinous. Mr T.H. Bryant, the Laxfield village schoolmaster, was elected local company Secretary.

The plans put forward at the end of 1898 were ambitious, providing for the construction of three lines totalling 50 miles in length, and including, with minor route changes, all those eventually built. The principal line of what were grandly termed the 'Mid-Suffolk Light Railways' was to run from the divergence of the GER Norwich and Bury St Edmunds lines at Haughley, in an easterly direction to the town of Halesworth, 27¾ miles away and already the junction between the GER East Suffolk line and the 3 ft gauge Southwold Railway, opened in 1879. A second line was to run from Westerfield, then and now the first station out of Ipswich on the East Suffolk line where, since 1877, the at first independent Felixstowe branch had broken away, to a junction with the first route at Kenton, 13½ miles to the north, 10 miles from Haughley and 17¾ from Halesworth. The final route proposed would connect with the GER at Needham Market, between Ipswich and Haughley, and run north-eastward for eight miles to Debenham, where it would join the Westerfield-Kenton line. The entire system would be single track, with a very few passing places.

Viewed as part of the national railway map, the system planned could be seen not only as providing local connections but, through the Haughley-Halesworth route, offering a more direct link from Cambridge and the Midlands to the East Coast than via either Ipswich or Norwich. But its essential purpose was to tap a sizeable hinterland reckoned to have a strong potential in agricultural traffic, with a scattered population approaching 15,000 (though much of it was two miles or more from the projected route of the line). It added only three communities with 1,000 or more inhabitants to the railway network: Mendlesham, Stradbroke and Debenham - the eventual terminus, Laxfield, at the time had a population of around 800. However the line as proposed would not only come within striking distance of Ipswich, in those days not yet a magnet for commuters, but give direct access to Halesworth, then with a population of just over 2,300, and at Haughley would be just a stop away from Stowmarket, a pocket of industry with some 4,300 inhabitants.

Connections and access to these last would, however, depend on the goodwill of the Great Eastern, and it soon became evident that this could not be taken for granted. Determined to protect its interests, the 'main line' company lodged a formal objection to the scheme at the outset. It feared that the Mid-Suffolk might seek and gain approval for running connections with the GER at each of the proposed junctions, not only impeding the working of that company's own trains but conceivably running over its lines to Ipswich and elsewhere with official *fiat*. The promoters of the Mid-Suffolk were quick to assure the Great Eastern that there were no such intentions, and to draft plans showing separate terminal stations at Haughley, Halesworth, Westerfield and Needham Market, with stock having to be shunted from one company's tracks to the other. When the plans were discussed at a hearing at the Board of Trade on 1st February, 1899 before Sir Courtenay Boyle, the Mid-Suffolk delegation (the promoters plus Mr Bryant and the company's solicitor) gave assurances that there would be 'no running connection' with the Great Eastern. It was pointed out that for through running to be practicable, parts of the existing stations at Halesworth and Haughley would have to be reconstructed (in the case of Haughley this was later disproved). Mr C.C. Hutchinson, counsel for the GER, acknowledged that the MSLR after early disagreements was now co-operating fully. But he told Sir Courtenay: 'It made us pretty well turn in our graves when we heard that they were endeavouring to make connections with our railways, and that is why we opposed them'.

Locally there was general support for the scheme, even if promises of hard cash were limited. Mr Stevenson took no chances that opposition on the ground might frustrate the project, holding meetings in villages along the course of the line to rally support and allay concern. He raised the prospect of the line both attracting new industry to the area and leading to greater prosperity in general. Six rural district councils and 40 parish councils welcomed the project, but there was strong opposition both to the principle and detail from Mendlesham parish council which, on 1st April, 1899, passed an outspoken resolution against the railway. All ten members present concurred that 'the proposed line was not desirable and is of no advantage to either landlord or tenant. The feeling of the meeting was that on account of the easy distance from Mendlesham to Stowmarket and Finningham (north of Haughley on the Norwich line) the line was unnecessary'. While this final sentence smacks of prophecy, one has to note that the resolution was moved by Mr F.J. Robinson of Park Farm, one of the most vocal objectors who was concerned that the trains would frighten working horses, and that the meeting was chaired by Mr George Barnes, another opponent of the project from the outset. By contrast, most landowners in the area saw the line as a boon, or at worst a minor inconvenience; once formal application for a Light Railway Order had been lodged on 1st May, 1899 and the route published in the *East Anglian Daily Times,* no others came out against it. The line was due to pass through the land of enough influential men to have strangled the project at birth had they chosen, among them Lords Henniker, Huntingfield, Tollemache and de Saumarez.

The inquiry, held at Ipswich Town Hall on 6th July with the Earl of Jersey in the chair, was concerned both with detailed representations over the course of the line and the fundamental question of whether the promoters either needed to build it at all or would be prudent to do so. On the first score, there were written representations from a handful of landowners seeking minor changes of course and from the villagers of Witnesham and Huntingfield pressing for their stations (neither of which was ever to be built) to be more conveniently sited. Mr F.W.H. Smith, for the promoters, grandly introduced the scheme as 'the most important to be brought before the Commissioners since the Light Railway Act of 1896'. He reported that agreement had been reached with the Great Eastern on junctions and the interchange of traffic - a point confirmed by Mr Hutchinson who stated that the GER had dropped its initial objections and now saw the Mid-Suffolk as a 'feeder'. Mr Smith did not directly address the question of the prudence of the scheme, but presented a petition signed by 4,141 local people in support and estimated that the entire 50 miles planned could be built for £240,000.

Yet the main question in the minds of the Light Railway Commissioners was indeed whether the promoters were overstretching themselves. Mr Stevenson agreed under questioning that the Needham Market line had been added as an afterthought, though some backers argued that it was essential to the overall scheme because of the maltings traffic it would attract. The Commissioners in due course reported that after hearing all the evidence they were 'of the opinion that an Order to authorise the main portion of the proposed railway from Halesworth to Westerfield should be made'. But they went on to request the promoters to 'consider whether they should press for both portions from

Bedingfield (Kenton) to Haughley, and from Debenham to Needham Market, or whether they would not be better advised to decide upon one of these portions, omitting the other for the present'. The Commissioners pointed out that to construct both these lines would add to the company's costs while contributing little to revenue.

The choice facing the promoters was more finely balanced than a glance at the map might suggest. The Needham Market line was shorter and, with no major earthworks, much less costly to construct, and served three communities of moderate size in Creeting St Mary, Earl Stonham and Stonham Aspall. That to Haughley was not only two miles longer but involved the construction of three bridges (one was later done without) and a lengthy cutting. With the exception of Mendlesham, the villages it served - Aspall, Brockford, Wetheringsett and Old Newton - were small, but the line did have the crucial advantage of terminating at a major junction with links not only to Ipswich but to the Midlands and the North via Bury. Had the Mid-Suffolk promoters known that the line was never to reach Westerfield, the Needham Market route would have offered the cheapest way of bringing it to a single junction with the GER on its way out of Ipswich, and assured Debenham of a place on the 'main' line. However, no-one at that stage doubted that the Westerfield line would be constructed.

Thus it was that the promoters of the line discarded the proposed Needham Market branch. The scheme as revised and outlined in the draft Light Railway Order considered by the Commissioners provided for a total of 42 route miles between Haughley and Halesworth, and Kenton and Westerfield, with a 'line to junction with siding' at each connecting point with the GER. There were to be eight bridges over roads (three of them on the approaches to Debenham) and five under them. Signals would only be installed at termini and crossing-places, of which there would be few. Locomotive weights would be heavily restricted: to 12 tons per axle if 56 lb. per yard rail were used, 14 tons if 60 lb. rail were laid. And while there was the standard 25 mph speed limit, it was further stipulated that locomotives running tender first (if tender engines were used) would be limited to 15 mph. There were even safeguards in the event of the line being electrified, the Light Railway Act also being the instrument under which many tramways were constructed. On a more realistic note, the plans deposited with the draft Order set the tone for the operation of the line by providing for almost 200 level crossings, the vast majority being 'occupation' crossings for use by farmers. The heaviest gradient on the 'main' line would be 1 in 60 (the plans as later revised included a short stretch at 1 in 42) and, on the Westerfield branch through more hilly terrain south of Debenham, 1 in 50. The curves were for the most part graded as 'easy', the tightest being 15 chains in radius.

The granting of a Light Railway Order depended heavily on the opinion of Col Sir Francis Marindin who, prior to his involvement with the Railway Inspectorate, had been a household name in a very different field. As a Captain in the Royal Engineers in 1871 he had been a member of the committee that devised the FA Cup competition, and duly played in the first final in which the Royal Engineers lost to Oxford University. He captained the side in 1874, again finishing on the losing side, and would have gained a winner's medal the following year against the Old Etonians had he not decided that, having been to Eton himself, it would be unsporting for him to take part. He went on to referee seven subsequent finals.

Sir Francis was an equal authority in the railway world, so the terms of his approval of the Mid-Suffolk scheme must have done much to commend it not only to the President of the Board of Trade but also to potential investors. Having reviewed the proposed route in detail, he concluded that it was 'one of the best projects that had come under his notice'. There was a last minute hitch when the Great Eastern complained that the draft Order did not comply with earlier agreements, but on 5th April, 1900 the Board of Trade duly granted the Light Railway Order. The Mid-Suffolk company was empowered to charge rates 25 per cent higher than those permitted the Great Eastern, on condition that they were to lapse if that company took over the line. In return the MSLR was required to maintain sidings at Haughley and Halesworth to the 'reasonable satisfaction' of the GER.

Having obtained approval for the line, Mr Stevenson and his associates set about forming a company to bring it into being. The Earl of Stradbroke, of Henham Hall, Wangford, the county's leading aristocrat, was brought on board as Vice-Chairman, and the Board was completed by Mr Kilby, Mr (later Sir) Daniel Ford Goddard, Liberal MP for Ipswich from 1895 to 1918, and Mr J.B. Chevallier of Aspall Hall, whose forebear had brought from Normany in 1728 the first apples for the celebrated Aspall cider press. Mr Kilby resigned almost straight away and Mr Goddard not long after, and at the close of 1901 two further local men of substance, Mr J.D. Cobbold of Holy Wells, Ipswich, a member of the great Suffolk brewing dynasty, and Mr F.M. Remnant of Wenhaston Grange, took their places; each was to lose heavily through his involvement with the company.

The Mid-Suffolk Light Railway Company incorporated in October 1900 was empowered to raise capital of £300,000, and chose to do so largely through debenture and preference shares, a decision which was to be a major cause of the undertaking's downfall. Within a month the Board began to suspect that the course being followed, while in line with the practice of the day, might not have been properly authorised, and went back to the Board of Trade for an Amendment Order giving it clear legal backing for the issue of preference shares. The company was duly authorised to issue half of its £225,000 capital in the form of preference shares, the dividend not to exceed 5 per cent; in the event £50,000 was raised in debenture stock at 4 per cent, and £75,210 in 4½ per cent preference shares; a further £18,910 in ordinary share capital was raised. Before work could begin, the Directors had to lodge securities of their own with the High Court, Mr Stevenson, the Earl of Stradbroke, Messrs Chevallier, Cobbold and Remnant subscribing £10,617 2s. 8d. between them. The plans put forward at the flotation of the company were essentially those approved in the Order, though minor adjustments to the route were made then and continued to be throughout the period of construction with the agreement of the Board of Trade to mollify objectors; the most notable were in the Mendlesham and Otley areas.

The company, in its Prospectus, also proposed to run (horse) buses from Westerfield station to the centre of Ipswich, in competition with Great Eastern

MID-SUFFOLK LIGHT RAILWAY

—— PLAN OF ——

Ground for Ceremony on

May 3rd 1902.

STORES

CENTRE LINE OF RAILWAY

STORES

LUNCHEON

TENT

BAND

BAND

ENCLOSURE FOR

PUBLIC

Duke's
Enclosure

CEREMONY

PUBLIC

PUBLIC ENTRANCE

Ladies
Cloak Room

Gentlemen

To Witnesham

WESTERFIELD ROAD

G.E. EASTERN R.Y.

UP PLATFORM

DOWN PLATFORM

To Felixstowe.

From Ipswich

F. S. Alger. Litho. Diss.

The ground plan prepared for the ceremony at Westerfield, showing the track layout at
Westerfield GER and the alignment proposed for the Mid-Suffolk Light Railway.

trains and presumably with Ipswich Corporation trams over part of the route. The service would have been convenient for some passengers from the line, as Ipswich station is well away from the town centre.

Promotion of the line was, needless to say, greeted with enthusiasm by the local Press, but there was some confusion about the precise purpose of the undertaking. The *East Anglian Daily Times*, published in Ipswich but circulating throughout the area, saw the line as running from Westerfield to Halesworth, with the Kenton-Haughley section having the status of a branch. The company perhaps inadvertently encouraged this by staging the ceremony of cutting the first sod at Westerfield because the venue would be more convenient for guests, when work had been under way at Haughley for several weeks. Yet its advertisements for this occasion depicted the Westerfield line as the branch, reinforcing the company's Prospectus which saw it as linking Ipswich with its hinterland, while building up the Haughley-Halesworth line as 'giving a direct route from Cambridge and the Midlands to the numerous popular seaside resorts on the East Coast'.

The genesis of the Mid-Suffolk was not helped by a an 18 month delay in starting work, caused by an inability to give the starting signal to the originally chosen contractors. On 5th July, 1900 S. Pearson and Son signed the contract to construct the line with an estimated completion date of December 1904, and in the normal course of events one could have expected work to begin shortly after. Yet by March the following year Pearson's were complaining that the Board had given them no instructions to commence, the delay stemming partly from the need to rectify the legal position before raising the necessary capital. Moreover surveys by Jeyes and Godden during 1901 revealed that while the Haughley-Halesworth line would for the most part be easier to construct, unexpectedly boggy ground on the approaches to Halesworth meant that that section of the line would have to be replanned. Pearson's repeatedly warned that they could not wait indefinitely, and soon after the Prospectus was finally issued in December 1901, they pulled out. A hasty search for a replacement led to S. Jackson and Co. of London and Doncaster being appointed to construct the line at a cost of £5,300 per mile, and on 11th January, 1902 they took on the task; prophetically the meeting at which Jackson's came on board also heard that problems were arising with landowners over the routing of the Westerfield branch, a second indication that the planning of the line had been less than thorough.

The ceremonial cutting of the first sod, the most colourful event in the history of the line save possibly for the wake half a century later, took place on 3rd May, 1902 in a field beside and below Westerfield GER station at the point where the line from Kenton was expected to terminate. It was crowned by the presence of HRH the Duke of Cambridge to wield the traditional shovel. The Duke, a well-preserved 83 years of age, was accompanied by military splendour recalling his tenure as Commander-in-Chief, the abrupt ending of which by Lord Rosebery's government seven years before had earned him the epithet 'poor George' from his cousin Queen Victoria and led to the Liberals being driven from office. (He clearly did not associate the Chairman of the Mid-Suffolk company with his removal.) Also present were a host of luminaries including the Marquis and Marchioness of Bristol, Lord Claud Hamilton, Chairman of the Great Eastern who gave his name to its most celebrated locomotives, Lord Rayleigh - who had recently chaired a Board of Trade inquiry into whether London's 'twopenny tube' (the Central Line) should be built - Lord Huntingfield, Sir Charles Dalrymple and Sir William Gateacre. The Duke, who arrived by special train from Liverpool Street and travelled on later to Orwell on the Felixstowe branch, told the gathering that the country should not go too fast; changes should be made gradually. 'We are too fond these days of rushing', he stated in terms which could have characterised the delays already dogging the construction of the line and the leisurely pace of travel on that portion which eventually opened. The speeches over, the Duke cut the first sod and deposited it in the highly ornate wheelbarrow, and just over 600 lucky holders of red and gilt lunch tickets sat down to a large meal in a spacious marquee equipped with six carving tables - a far grander pavilion than ever adorned any of the Mid-Suffolk's working stations.

A NEW LIGHT RAILWAY IN EAST ANGLIA: THE DUKE OF CAMBRIDGE CUTTING THE FIRST SOD OF THE MID-SUFFOLK LINE.

A contemporary sketch of the ceremony at Westerfield, with the Duke of Cambridge wielding the silver shovel. Mr Stevenson, the company Chairman, is right of centre.

Once again reaction from the Press was lyrical, the *East Anglian Daily Times* being inspired to comment on 5th May: 'Into the night of mid-Suffolk, Mr F.S. Stevenson has flung the stone - has been the principal means of starting a light railway'. This allusion to a well-known line in the *Rubaiyat of Omar Khayyam*, which had been translated by the Suffolk poet Fitzgerald, was again prophetic, in that it brought into focus the remoteness of the line and the dreamlike character of its objectives. What the writer inspired by the ceremony could not know was that the scene of such splendour would never see track, let alone trains, that it would be six long years before even a portion of the line was fully open, and that two of the Directors standing beside the Duke would be virtually beggared by the undertaking.

The fiction that work was under way on the Westerfield branch was maintained by Jackson's deputing a few men to clear the station site, but the serious effort was in hand at Haughley, where the company had asked the contractor to proceed 'as expeditiously as possible'. Work there had begun in March, and by the time the festivities took place at Westerfield the site of Haughley exchange sidings had been cleared and work was well advanced on the Haugh Lane bridge. Before long a rail connection was in place to a gravel pit close to the new line a few hundred yards out from Haughley where ballast for it was quarried, and throughout 1902 work proceeded apace. Altogether 200 navvies were at work on the line, with construction methods little different from the early days of the railway age. Earthworks were constructed through the agency of horses pulling tip trucks along lengths of 2 ft gauge track; this was replaced for service trains by flat-bottomed 'Vignoles' rail in 30 ft lengths, weighing 56 lb. per yard and laid with staggered joints, on half-round sleepers.

By the end of July four miles of track had been laid, and on 23rd September General Viscount Kitchener was able to pay an official visit to the line and travel on it from Brockford - fittingly now the home of the revived Mid-Suffolk - to Haughley. The train comprised contractor's wagons and a GER saloon, and was hauled by the Manning, Wardle saddle tank *Lady Stevenson*, named after the company Chairman's mother. Needless to say, the great day did not go quite as planned. Kitchener had spent the night at Aspall after a reception at Ipswich, and went on by road to the line. He called first at Mendlesham where schoolgirls cheered him as he left his car, then drove to Brockford station. Canon E.W. Blythe, then a boy of 14, was among the locals who gathered on the platform after hearing that the great man was coming to take 'the first ride on the new railway'.

At last Kitchener arrived but there was no train, the Canon recalled in the 1960s. 'He walked up and down in what little space was left for what seems, looking back, to have been a good 20 minutes. His annoyance was increased by some of the spectators pushing through the crowd and catching hold of his coat-tails so that they could say that they had "touched Kitchener"'. After a while the train came in and he went off.

The official train duly made its way to Haughley, six miles away, where Lord Kitchener drank a glass of champagne and presumably steadied his nerves before setting off with a cortege of horseless carriages to cover the three miles to Stowmarket by road.

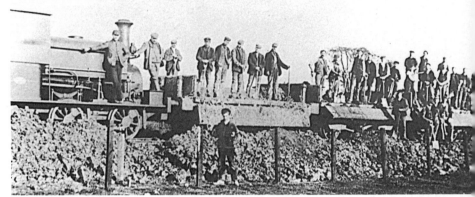

A contractor's train hauled by Jackson's first locomotive, probably photographed near Mendlesham - September 1902. *MSLR Co.*

A preference share certificate issued by the Mid-Suffolk company. *Public Record Office*

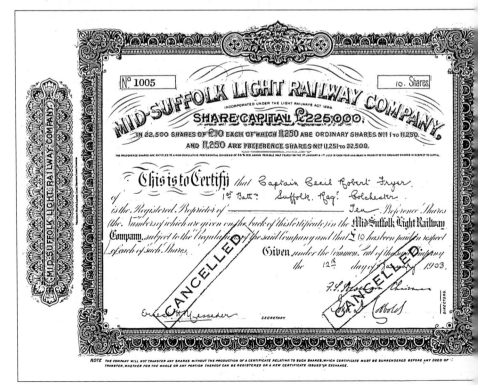

Bearing in mind that the company's records tell of the distinguished visitor having been borne from Mendlesham to Haughley, Canon Blythe asked:

Was there by any chance a muddle? Was the train waiting for him at Mendlesham and he waiting for it at Brockford and Wetheringsett? Mendlesham, being the larger place, was more likely to have been chosen for the event, but he certainly did start from Brockford and I have a vivid recollection of the coat-tail episode.

On the face of it, construction of the line was living up to the Board's best hopes. In February 1903 the local Press reported satisfaction in the neighbourhood of Worlingworth, Stradbroke and Laxfield at the pegging out of the course of the line from Kenton to Halesworth. By mid-March it as complete as far as Kenton and the company was urging Jackson's to press ahead with the lines from there to Halesworth and to Westerfield, 'but more rapidly towards the former than towards the latter'. On 11th July, 1903 a train bringing navvies and stores from Haughley to the edge of Laxfield also carried passengers including senior management of Jackson's, and two days later a special train comprising a GER saloon and wagons ran from Haughley to Mendlesham, where it picked up Mr Stevenson and the band of the Forresters and conveyed them to Horham over eight miles of the line which had not been completed the previous September. The track beyond Horham was also laid, but as it had yet to settle fully the party transferred to a contractor's train for the five miles to Laxfield. This time, there is no record of any hitch in the arrangements. After this, such trains had to be suspended as the contractor got down to the major task of replacing the temporary embankment and crossing of the Ipswich-Norwich road at Mendlesham with a cutting and bridge; to keep work moving ahead on the rest of the line, supplies were stockpiled at Kenton.

Halesworth, however, was still 8¾ miles away from the railhead, and events the day after Mr Stevenson's excursion were to demonstrate that all was far from well with the company's plans to reach it. Doubts over the original approach to the town over marshy ground had led the Mid-Suffolk to apply in November 1901 for an Order authorising a diversion. The new line would be one mile shorter and take a totally different route, diverging some 24 miles from Haughley to skirt Halesworth on the north-western side and terminate to the north, rather than the south, of the Great Eastern station. A one furlong spur would make a trailing connection with the main line. The hearing of the company's application was held at the Angel Hotel, Halesworth, on 14th July, 1903 under Col Boughey and Mr H.A. Steward. The Great Eastern objected on the ground that goods trains would have to be exchanged on a gradient of 1 in 70 (1 in 96 according to counsel for the Mid-Suffolk) and trains leaving the light railway would have to cross both GER running lines to reach the main sidings. Despite the objections, the application for the new route into Halesworth was granted and work began on the considerable earthworks required before the company began to wonder if it had bitten off more than it could chew. In due course another, and somewhat bizarre, proposal for gaining access to Halesworth was to be put forward before the MSLR Board concluded that the northern route was in fact their best and only hope.

Other storm clouds were gathering: relations between the Board and Jackson's were getting steadily worse, and the money was running out. No wonder that when the Chairman of Kenton parish council wrote to the company proposing extensions to meet the GER at Eye, Framlingham and Saxmundham it had to reply that there was no intention of doing so. The quarrels with the contractor were over many things: fences not erected, light and heavy work done together instead of separately as planned and failure to provide a water supply for the locomotives. For their part, Jackson's must have been confused by changes in the route required once work had begun, and by their inability to start at Westerfield because of continued squabbles with the Great Eastern over the best form of connection between the two systems.

The situation was in fact deteriorating rapidly. The Board wanted the Haughley-Laxfield and Kenton-Debenham sections open by the end of September 1904, but the bulk of the capital had been spent with only half the projected line completed. In January of that year the refusal of the Mid-Suffolk company's local bankers to extend further credit had forced the Board to raise bonds at Lloyd's. Legal action was considered against the contractor who had still not finished the cutting at Mendlesham, but in May 1904 the company's need for cash was so acute that it made a direct approach to East Suffolk County Council for a loan of £25,000 which it reckoned would suffice to complete the lines to Westerfield and Halesworth. The proposal, which would have required a two-thirds majority, was defeated by 27 votes to 24, an outcome which played its part in ensuring that the line was not to be completed.

Nevertheless, Mr Stevenson remained outwardly optimistic, assuring the annual shareholders' meeting in July 1904 that the lines to Laxfield and Debenham would open on schedule and that the Halesworth section would be ready the following February. He referred to arrangements being made with the GER for covered ways to connect the two companies' stations at Westerfield and Halesworth, and to the planned use of steam rail motors for passenger services, drawing from the Taff Vale Railway's experience the conclusion that operating costs would be 5½d. per mile. The Chairman told the meeting that the contractor was working on the bridge over the Aspall Road just north of Debenham, and that fencing was being done as far as Linstead (3½ miles beyond Laxfield) on the 'main' line and Otley (4¾ miles short of Westerfield) on the branch.

However, the contractor was making a meal of work on the 2½ miles of line into Debenham which included substantial earthworks. At this time Jackson's had their offices at Debenham and Mr Frederick Moore, who worked on the construction of the line, told the *East Anglian* that he used to lodge in a cottage on the Aspall Road and was picked up every morning by a train comprising the contractor's locomotive *Lady Stevenson*, some wagons and a pay office converted from an open wagon. Though this section of line was tantalisingly close to completion, it became clear that it would not be ready on time. The Board thus decided that both the company and its potential customers had waited long enough, and announced that the 19 miles from Haughley to Laxfield would open for goods traffic from 20th September, 1904.

Chapter Two

Opening for Freight
and Financial Crisis

It would have been too much to expect the opening of the first section of the line for goods traffic to pass off without incident. To provide the advertised service, the Mid-Suffolk company needed at least one of the two locomotives it had ordered from Hudswell, Clarke of Leeds, but at the very last moment the manufacturer's got wind of the line's financial difficulties. The first engine was delivered to Haughley, but kept chained and padlocked to the rails there until Hudswell, Clarke had received the first instalment of the purchase price. The locomotive, ironically named *Haughley*, was then released, though not in time to haul the first scheduled trains which for at least the fortnight until the manufacturer's delivery date of 5th October were operated by the contractor's *Lady Stevenson*. With even greater irony, the company was within a few months to use the unchained engine as security to raise a loan.

The Mid-Suffolk Board had carried out a survey of potential freight traffic and convinced itself that the long term prospects were good. It was thus quite prepared to wait until the entire system was completed before inaugurating a passenger service, duly arranging for livestock, freight and parcels to be carried in the meantime. Provision of a passenger service would also require a Board of Trade inspection and this was far from a formality, as the company would discover to its cost. Mr Stevenson had told the Mid-Suffolk Board that a freight service could be run 'with seven men', but operations began with several times that number on the payroll, even though intermediate stations were initially staffed only when a goods train was actually calling.

The first scheduled train left Haughley at 8.00 am on Tuesday 20th September, 1904, behind *Lady Stevenson* and arrived at Laxfield, 19 miles away, at 11.15 after stops at Mendlesham, Aspall, Kenton, Horham and Stradbroke. Of the 3 hours 15 minutes the journey was advertised to take, a full 1 hour 33 minutes was allowed for shunting at intermediate stations. On the inaugural run this was hardly needed; the only freight carried was ballast for the contractor, though several parcels were picked up on the return journey which left Laxfield at 1.00 pm and reached Haughley at 4.15. Some of the slack in an over-generous schedule was taken up in the months that followed as stops were added at Old Newton,* Brockford, Worlingworth and Wilby. By January 1905, the company was reporting a monthly traffic of 1,500 tons of freight, 30 trucks of cattle and 500 parcels. At this time an early train for the Ipswich cattle market was introduced, connecting to leave Haughley at 4.30 am; while the area was turning from cattle to corn and this traffic did not develop as hoped, the train ran for 30 years, later leaving Laxfield at 3.50 am. The availability of a railhead for cattle from the Laxfield area was felt sharply by the GER in a loss of traffic by its Framlingham branch, to which the beasts had previously been herded by road.

---

* Either the short-lived Brown Street siding where a passenger station named Old Newton was contemplated, or less probably Gipping siding which also began handling freight traffic after the opening of the line and was never intended to do more.

OPENING OF THE LINE FOR GOODS TRAFFIC.

For the convenience of the Public, and as a temporary arrangement, it has been decided to OPEN PART OF THIS LINE for **Goods, Live Stock, and Parcels Traffic,**

On TUESDAY, September 20th, 1904,

When the following Stations will be available, viz :—

HAUGHLEY	**HORHAM**
MENDLESHAM	**STRADBROKE**
ASPALL	**LAXFIELD**
KENTON	

Your attention is particularly directed to the fact that at present the *Stations will only be open at specified times,* as per accompanying Time Table, and that Traffic can only be dealt with at those times.

Trucks will be left at the various Stations, and can be unloaded at once.

Advise. Notes of Traffic awaiting delivery will be sent to Consignees.

A List of Parcels awaiting delivery will be displayed at each Station.

Particulars can be obtained from the Officials at the time the Trains are at the various Stations, or from

MR. H. L. GODDEN, General Manager, FRAMSDEN Stowmarket.

MR. H. J. REDNALL, Traffic Manager, HAUGHLEY, Stowmarket.

MR. H. R. GILLINGWATER, Assistant Manager, HAUGHLEY, Stowmarket

Mr. T. H. BRYANT, Local Secretary, LAXFIELD, Framlingham.

TIME TABLE.

		A.M.			P.M.
HAUGHLEY,	.... depart	8.0	**LAXFIELD,**	.... depart	1.0
Mendlesham,	.... arrive	8.20	**Stradbroke,**	.... arrive	1.15
	.... depart	8.40		.... depart	1.35
Aspall, ...	.... arrive	9.5	**Horham,**	.... arrive	1.42
....	.... depart	9.25	....	.... depart	2.2
Kenton, ...	.... arrive	9.30	**Kenton,**	.... arrive	2.32
....	.... depart	9.45	....	.... depart	2.47
Horham, ...	.... arrive	10.15	**Aspall,**	.... arrive	2.52
....	.... depart	10.35	...	.... depart	3.12
Stradbroke,	.... arrive	10.42	**Mendlesham,**	.... arrive	3.36
	.... depart	11.0		.... depart	3.55
LAXFIELD,	.... arrive	11.15	**HAUGHLEY,**	.... arrive	4.15

A handbill announcing the opening of the line to freight traffic.

Before much longer, trains were running half a mile beyond Laxfield station to Goram's Mill, or Laxfield Mills as the siding there was officially known. The first portion of this brief extension may have been used from the outset so that locomotives could take on water from a conveniently sited pond, given the disputes with the contractor over the firm's failure to lay on a proper water supply. The Mid-Suffolk company had purchased land for the further extension of the line from the proprietor of the mill on condition that a service was operated there in perpetuity. It is probable that the first freight train reached the mill siding late in 1904 or early the following year; the 91-year-old widow of Walter Flatman, for many years porter at Wilby, recalled in 1995 her mother telling her how she had been lifted up to her bedroom window in Laxfield when a baby to see it pass.

A service of sorts was also being provided on the Debenham branch, even though work on it had slowed to a snail's pace, leaving the rails a tantalising 150 yards short of the centre of the village. It is usually stated - even in the LNER's post-Grouping records - that no part of the Westerfield line was opened or traffic of any kind handled, but some freight was indeed conveyed to and from Debenham in the line's earliest days, and the likely site of loading can be identified. Whether the trucks were hauled to and from Kenton by *Lady Stevenson*, the more likely means given the incomplete state of the line, or whether the Mid-Suffolk's own locomotives sauntered down the branch during the time allowed for shunting at the junction, will probably never be known.

The first of these locomotives, *Haughley*, was intended for freight traffic and market specials, with the second to supplement it on lighter duties. In the first few months of operation the Mid-Suffolk had to hire wagons from the Great Eastern, as those it had ordered had yet to be delivered. By the company's 1905 annual meeting, it could be reported that both engines were now in service, together with seven carriages, two brake vans, two horse boxes, six cattle wagons and 18 open trucks.

The senior officials of the company at the time of opening to freight traffic were Mr Godden (the original Engineer of the line, now traffic manager), Mr H.J. Rednal (assistant manager), Mr H.R. Gillingwater (superintendent from 1904), and Mr Bryant (local Secretary). Mr Rednal and Mr Gillingwater were each paid £100 a year; Mr Bryant, who apparently regarded association with the new railway as its own reward, was censured by the education authorities for neglecting his schoolmasterly duties at Laxfield. From 1905 Mr C.D. Szlumper, of the family firm of consulting railway engineers founded by Sir James Weekes Szlumper, pioneer of such varying schemes as the Lynton and Barnstaple Railway and the embryo Piccadilly Line, was retained as Engineer to the Mid-Suffolk; Mr T.J. Dalgleish, a Scot whose involvement with the line was to continue until the Grouping, was assistant engineer and accountant. The post of company Secretary at the London offices in Old Broad Street of W.H. Smith and Sons, the MSLR's solicitors, changed hands frequently, Mr N.P. Jaffrey being followed in February 1902 by Mr Ernest Messeder, one of the practice's clerks. He in turn resigned two years later, after which Mr W. Warren served as acting Secretary.

Mr Gillingwater emerged early as the moving spirit of the line in the face of

Locomotive No. 1 pauses at Kenton with a short goods train bound for Haughley in the line's earliest days. The station is shown in its original form, before the changes ordered by the Board of Trade after the adverse report on the inspection carried out in July 1905.

H.C. Casserley Collection

Locomotive No. 2, normally preferred for passenger work, posed at Haughley in 1907 with the train of cattle wagons used on the early Tuesday morning market special for Ipswich. The train has halted on Haugh Lane bridge with the locomotive on the points running into the MSLR yard; behind on the running line is the original shed, whose removal was ordered two years previously.

L&GRP

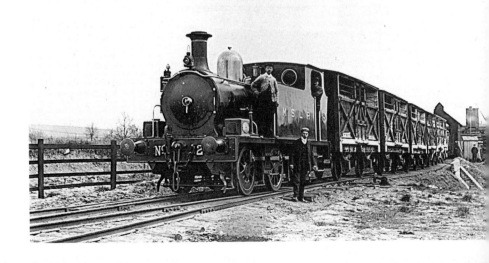

all its difficulties. The son of the station master at Diss, he had learned his trade with the Lancashire, Derbyshire and East Coast Railway prior to its absorption into the Great Central, and made full use of his experience of a line that had been left incomplete to get the Mid-Suffolk into operation with first a freight and then a passenger service as the pillars crashed around him. *The Locomotive* of 15th May, 1907 described him as having acted with 'commendable energy' to make the line serve the needs of the community.

Optimism was still the keynote at the first annual staff dinner held in mid-February, 1905 at the Queen's Head, Stradbroke, prior to which the Press were given a conducted tour of the line in goods vehicles. At this stage the 20 ft deep cutting to take the line under the Ipswich-Norwich road was still incomplete and trains had to tackle a stiff ascent to a temporary level crossing. The diversion was completed in June 1905, around which time the Ipswich Scientific Society toured the line, apparently travelling - at their own risk - over both the contractor's line and the route that was to replace it. Both the company's locomotives were called into action with some highly irregular working on a day that took the enthusiasts as far as Laxfield in one of the line's otherwise unused ex-Metropolitan carriages, coupled to a GER brake. The *East Anglian Daily Times* reported that the passengers were 'no worse for the experience, if one excepts two or three adventurous spirits who missed the return train at Laxfield'. One would love to know how they got home, given that it would be three more years before the first scheduled passenger train.

With the diversion near Mendlesham complete, the MSLR Board must have been confident that work could be concentrated on new construction to complete the system. However the Directors hedged their bets by deciding to apply to the Board of Trade to operate a passenger service over the route thus far constructed, instead of waiting until the line reached Halesworth. Sadly for them, the inspection conducted on 2nd July, 1905 by Lt-Col P.G. von Donop drove yet another nail into the coffin. He concluded that the line was unfit as it stood for passenger traffic, and that a further £5,000 would have to be spent on rectifying a raft of deficiencies and irregularities. These included the removal of the engine shed from the running line at Haughley, the lifting of connections there to sheds and the gravel pit, reconstruction of the line at Kenton to serve adequately as the line's only crossing place, and track to be realigned at four locations including the provision of trap points on the 'main' line out of Laxfield station. The report was a body-blow to the company which had been confident everything was in order. It brought a parting of the ways with Jeyes and Godden, who had planned the line and supervised its construction; they were dismissed on 25th September, 1905. It also brought to a head the already strained relations between the company and Jackson's, and the contractor was also discharged after failing to rectify the faults within a three month deadline. Arbitration followed which brought some financial relief to the company.

The very same day the company dropped its pilots, Mr Stevenson contrived to present a confident picture to the annual shareholders' meeting, reporting that revenue had been covering running expenses since the previous December. The Directors' confidence in completing the line was buttressed by their success in extracting a loan of £5,000 from Halesworth council, to whom they had gone

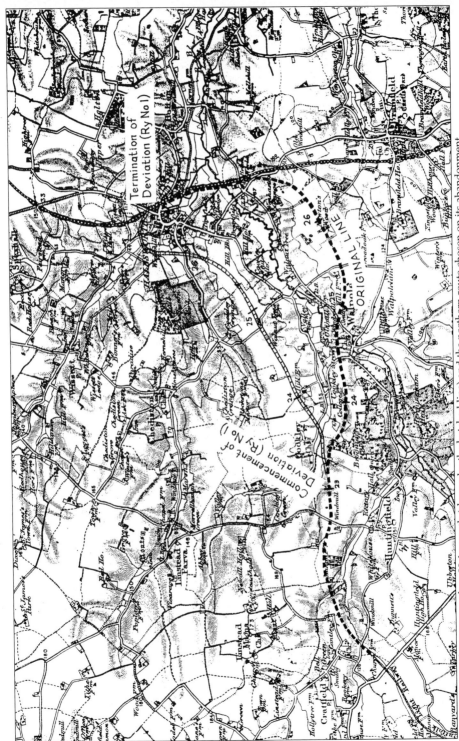

Termination of Deviation (Ry No 1)

ORIGINAL LINE

Commencement of Deviation (Ry No 1)

The original southern approach to Halesworth (shown by the hatched line) and the northern route chosen on its abandonment.
Reproduced from the 1″, 1906 Ordnance Survey Map

cap-in-hand. The loan, to have been backed by a similar sum from the Treasury, was unfortunately blocked by the company's debenture holders; the edifice was starting to topple.

The fall, when it came, was as spectacular as it was sudden, all the more so because the railway emerged as instrumental in the personal tragedy of its Chairman. In January 1906 Mr Stevenson, amid not a hint of scandal, was re-elected MP for Eye; in March he resigned his seat by applying for the Chiltern Hundreds and gave up the chairmanship of the company with equal haste and no explanation, and in May he was declared bankrupt, rendering worthless £20,000 in promissory notes and making the railway's financial position even more precarious.

From the public examination that ensued, it transpired that Mr Stevenson had lost some £95,000 of his own money in the promotion of the line. The ordinary shares were now selling at 57s. 6d. per £10, and debentures were withdrawn at an auction at this time after the biggest offer was £57. Moreover Mr Stevenson apparently agreed to purchase £100,000 of Great Eastern stock with the object of bringing about friendly relations between that company and the Mid-Suffolk, and had lost £30,000 on the deal. As the GER had suspected he was acting as a stalking-horse for the voracious Midland Railway to give it an entrée to the East Coast, this heavy investment was presumably intended to reassure the GER about his loyalties. The fact that the Mid-Suffolk company was seeking in its latest application to reach Halesworth, a junction with the Southwold line, which, after a change of gauge, could give it access to a coastal port, merely heightened the Great Eastern's concern and upped the stakes for Mr Stevenson. The knowledge that the Mid-Suffolk Chairman had also been dealing in Midland shares and would not explain why, forced those stakes still higher.

Mr Stevenson told his creditors frankly that he had been living on his wife's income since 1889, and on money left him by his stepfather. He described himself as never having been in business, having spent the greater part of his life in study and in publishing certain works, the copyright of which was of no value. He also agreed that in the final stages he was buying jewellery on credit and pawning it the same day; this exercise, and payments to money-lenders, had lost him a further £45,000. The Official receiver felt moved to tell him: 'You put all your eggs in one basket, and other people's as well'. Indeed he had even realised his mother's trust fund. Sympathy for a man in such straits is natural, but how could the fortunes of a railway have been given over to someone of such spectacular inadequacy in business? The answer must be that the scheme was his, and that local connections were all; this MP for Eye with his big house at Woodbridge was easily acceptable. Mr Stevenson, hailed as 'Father of the Mid-Suffolk', continually declared that he had accepted control of the company with reluctance, and he may indeed have regarded the job as an obligation. Although he had purchased land at Kenton, nothing came out to suggest that he had put his own interests before that of the railway. It must be remembered, too, that MPs were still unpaid when the bankruptcy occurred.

At the 1906 general meeting of the company, the forecasts from the new Chairman, the Earl of Stradbroke, were more subdued than previously. When a questioner asked about the prospects of opening the line from Debenham to

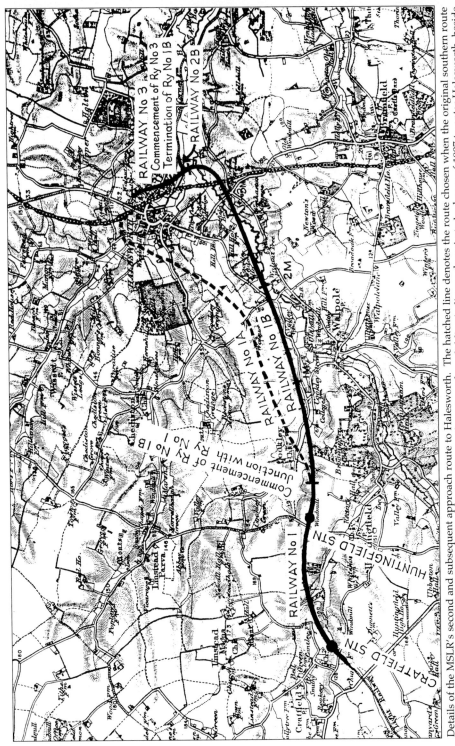

RAILWAY No 3
Commencement of Ry No 3
Termination of Ry No 1B

RAILWAY No 2B

RAILWAY No 1A

RAILWAY No 1B

2M

Commencement of Ry No 1B
Junction with Ry No 1

HUNTINGFIELD STN

RAILWAY No 1

CRATFIELD STN

Details of the MSLR's second and subsequent approach route to Halesworth. The hatched line denotes the route chosen when the original southern route was abandoned, dropped in turn because of the rejected scheme of 1907 to enter Halesworth, beside the earthworks. The solid line indicates the rejected scheme of 1907 to enter Halesworth, beside the earthworks. *Reproduced from the 1", 1906 Ordnance Survey Map of the Southwold Railway.*

Westerfield, he was told that 'they had better try to get to Halesworth first'. Reading between the lines, it looks as though work had virtually stopped.

The Board of Trade's refusal to let passenger services commence left the railway with a number of carriages for which it had no immediate and regular use (it had by now given up the idea of operating steam railcars) and a stretch of track beyond Laxfield Mills which had been in place for a year without even a freight service. The company thus decided to make the best of things by extending operations during 1906 over the mile and a half to Cratfield, where a siding and station building were already *in situ*. Yet if the most was being made of the 'main line', the Board - as the Earl had hinted - was now taking a decidedly sanguine view of the chances of reaching Westerfield. Hence the decision about this time, strongly objected to locally, to suspend the informal facility to 'load and unload' freight at Debenham.

February 1907 brought further evidence that the Mid-Suffolk would be hard pressed to reach Halesworth, in the form of a hearing into its second application to change the route into the town. The scale and expense of the civil engineering works required to bring the line in from the north had proved too much for the company's limited resources and it had concluded, wrongly as it turned out, that it would be best to write off the work already done and find a less costly solution. Telling the Light Railway Commissioners that it had been badly advised by its recently dispensed with engineers, the Mid-Suffolk company now asked for a third alternative to be accepted, namely of approaching the town from the south by a similar route to that originally proposed and approved, but then crossing the main East Suffolk line and running by the Southwold Railway for half a mile before branching off into a separate station just to the east of the GER and narrow gauge platforms.

Counsel for the Great Eastern showed considerable alarm at this proposal, for reasons which can be easily understood. The plans showed a triangular junction with the Southwold line (despite the difference of gauge) on the final stages of the approach to Halesworth, and the GER, bearing in mind the former Mid-Suffolk Chairman's dealings in Midland Railway shares, was only too clear what this might mean. The Mid-Suffolk's counsel was at pains to stress that his clients had no intention of running along the Southwold's tracks, save with that company's approval (and the Southwold were objectors). At this time there was talk of developing the River Blyth at Walberswick, 6½ miles from Halesworth and two from Southwold, as a major port; indeed in 1915 the Blackshore Quay was opened on the Southwold side of the river and a short-lived branch of the narrow gauge line constructed to serve it. The Great Eastern's counsel painted a lurid picture of this 'port' open, with a facing junction with the Mid-Suffolk at Halesworth, from a Southwold Railway converted to standard gauge and fish traffic pouring onto the line. It required little further imagination to see Southwold becoming another Harwich within the Midland empire - a spectre which haunted the Great Eastern Board all too vividly. The nearest Midland tracks might be at Huntingdon, but the company had running rights on to Cambridge and had once attempted to reach Felixstowe via Chesterton, Stradishall, Lavenham, Westerfield and the independent Felixstowe Railway opened in 1877.

The hearing brought out not only the practical difficulties the Mid-Suffolk faced in gaining access to Halesworth, but also the implications for its future in failing to do so. The company's counsel pointed out to the Commissioners that, with the line uncompleted, it had a railway 'from an ascertained point to a dead end', on which it could carry only freight traffic. This was showing a profit of £500 per annum and was steadily increasing, but the debenture interest was in arrears, a situation which could not be allowed to continue for long. Applications had been made for loans from local authorities, but the Commissioners would only allow them to be made if the debenture holders permitted them to rank *pari passu* with their own shares. This the holders, in keeping with their previous reluctance to see their already precarious position eroded still further even at the expense of a chance to guarantee the company's future, refused to do. After allowing interest to be held over for a further six months, the largest debenture holder, the Eagle Insurance Company, applied to the courts for a Receiver to be appointed, putting the Mid-Suffolk company under the tightest form of financial discipline.

In May 1907 a Receiver and Manager were called in, following proceedings in which the debenture holders even demanded proof that members of the company's Board at the time construction began had lodged the substantial bond required of them. It was reckoned at this time that the company, which had never succeeded in exercising its right to borrow £75,000 on top of maximum share capital of £225,000, had unsecured creditors pressing for payment of debts totalling some £30,000. Initially Mr Warren, the acting company Secretary, took on the responsibilities of Receiver, but he returned to his secretarial duties (which he was to continue until his death in 1912) when a specialist in the field was found. The post required someone with personal experience of operating a railway on a shoestring, and the task fell to Major J.F.R. Daniel, who had been one of the moving spirits behind the Weston, Clevedon and Portishead Railway, opened between 1897 and 1907.

Major Daniel, who had 'retired' as far back as 1892 as Manager of the Midland and South Western Junction Railway, was already 78 years of age when he took up responsibility for the Mid-Suffolk. But he was not only to retain the position for eleven years until his death in 1918, but would demonstrate the vigour and judgement needed to keep the line afloat. His remit was to restore financial soundness, to complete the line if practicable and, regardless of whether this were achieved, to fulfil the intention of its promoters by getting a passenger service started. The Major is said to have succeeded in putting together a financial package sufficient to complete the line, but in a short time a decision was taken to halt construction work, precious little of which had actually been done in the previous 2½ years. All immediate efforts were concentrated on preparing as much of the line as practicable for a fresh Board of Trade inspection so that passenger trains could at last begin to run. Mr Gillingwater, by now the line's manager as well as its superintendent, set to work with his staff on the ground on upgrading the track and station facilities, and on Friday 25th September, 1908, Lt-Col von Donop made a second inspection. This time he was more impressed, though he did remark on the poor quality of the ballast and ordered a handful of other minor improvements before passenger trains could run. Word that the Board of Trade had at last given its approval reached Laxfield the day after; the energetic Mr Gillingwater at once ordered the printing of posters announcing that passenger trains would start running between Haughley and Laxfield the following Tuesday; and over the weekend thousands of handbills publicising the service were distributed in villages close to the line. At long last the Mid-Suffolk Light Railway, or at least a substantial part of it, was to be fully in business.

A panoramic view of the full stretch of Brockford and Wetheringsett station taken from the south. Compare the appearance of the resurrected station on page 4.   *Lens of Sutton*

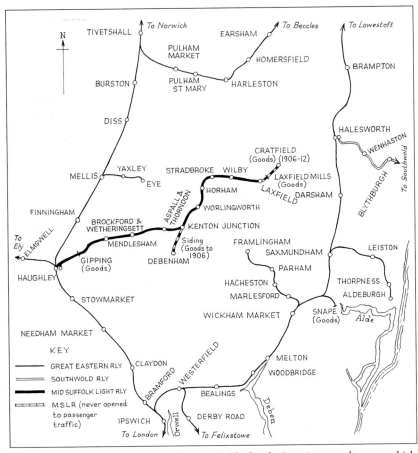

A map of the line as constructed and opened. The hatched sections are those on which scheduled passenger trains never ran. Note that reference to Old Newton station has disappeared; Wilby station is now shown, as is Laxfield Mills.

The very first ticket to be issued at Laxfield, as purchased by Mr F.M. Remnant, a Director of the Mid-Suffolk.   *Courtesy P.T.W. Remnant*

Chapter Three

Passengers at Last

To a fanfare of exploding detonators and cheers from the local populace, the first advertised passenger train on what rapidly became known as the 'Middy' left Laxfield for Haughley shortly after its scheduled departure time of 7.35 am on Tuesday 29th September, 1908. Major Daniel, the Receiver, had travelled down from London with his wife to make the first journey, and one of the company's surviving Directors, Mr Remnant, actually purchased the first ticket. Mr Chevallier, the other Director said by the local Press to have 'stuck to his post all through the troublous times' (though he did not lose his shirt like Mr Remnant and the Earl of Stradbroke), was also aboard, his family waiting on Aspall station to see him pass through.

The *East Anglian Daily Times* reported the day thus:

A good number of tickets were taken, and passengers were eager to enter the train. Only a few minutes behind time the signal was given by the Laxfield station master, and off the train steamed to the accompaniment of hearty cheers from the crowd on the platform, supplemented by the discharging of nearly thirty fog signals. It was a beautiful, bright morning, and the pleasure and satisfaction which these first travellers on the line derived from their journey was reflected in their faces. As Stradbroke was approached, heads popped out of many windows, and a sharp lookout was kept for friends who might be out to greet the train. More passengers were taken on, and once more the train was 'under way', leaving many smiling faces and waving hands behind. At all the other stations on the line - Horham, Worlingworth, Aspall, Brockford and Mendlesham - there were the same quiet signs of rejoicing, and while fresh passengers were secured, some alighted, having satisfied themselves that it was a real train, and that it really would convey them in a few minutes for a very trifling sum to the next village, which had always seemed so far away. All along the line at the various stations, the approach of the train was heralded by fog signals. At Brockford, quite a large number of schoolchildren entered the train to travel to school at Mendlesham, which is a mile and a half distant, and no doubt the 'nippers' will be glad, especially on wet days, to avail themselves of the new means of travelling.

(It was not long before the line's elderly stock earned a reputation among local schoolchildren as a propagator of scarlet fever.)

At Haughley, the other terminus, where the line adjoins that of the GER, Mr Kelly, the station master, resplendent in his new uniform, was all in readiness to receive the train, which arrived around three minutes late, and here it was a case of 'All Change'. Many went to some destination beyond, principally to Ipswich, but others awaited the next train back to Laxfield and intermediate stations, which left at 10 o'clock. A few flags were flying at Haughley station, which looked particularly smart with its freshly gravelled platform and clean paint, and several from the village came to see the train arrive, and inspected the empty carriages with great interest.

The Company possess six long carriages, which all communicate one with the other through the centre, a saloon, two horse boxes, parcels vans and brake vans, in addition to the usual trucks for merchandise. There are two excellent engines. The train has a

Quite a crowd at Stradbroke station in its very earliest days. Were they posing for the camera or awaiting the arrival of a train from Laxfield? *Lens of Sutton*

MSLR locomotive No. 2 coasts into Mendlesham station with a train for Laxfield. One wonders if the passengers were travelling for the fun of it, before the novelty wore off. *Lens of Sutton*

decidedly smart appearance, and the same can be said of the officials, whose new uniforms did not pass unnoticed amongst their friends and acquaintances. On the whole the new line starts under good auspices, and all interested wish it great success. The running of the trains was particularly smooth, which shows that the track has been well and truly laid.

The other trains from Laxfield at 10 am and 3.30 pm* had good complements of passengers, and so far as could be heard no hitch whatever occurred in connection with the opening day.

Today (Wednesday) the first and only excursion of the season will take place, this being a trip to Felixstowe at very cheap rates, and all Mid-Suffolk promises to disport itself at that popular watering place.

What the writer could not anticipate in his understandably fulsome account was that at least two of those present at the celebrations would also be there almost 44 years later to see the final train on the original 'Middy' pass the same way. Among the younger members of a party of Laxfield school children was Willis Keeble, who would join the line in 1917 and make over 30,000 trips on it as a guard, including the very last scheduled train. One other participant in both events was Mr A. Mayfield, a schoolmaster who was among the throng on the platform at Mendlesham to see the first train come in. He would be standing in the very same place, aged 78, to watch the last one leave.

Reports of the opening of the line to passengers stressed the dual role it could serve in bringing visitors to the area from outside and in giving its inhabitants greater mobility.

That there will be considerable desire on the part of the public at large to make the acquaintance of such places as Mendlesham, Stradbroke and Laxfield goes without saying, and the shareholders of the MSLR will say 'the more the merrier',

said the *East Anglian Daily Times*.

And although it is to most people a simple matter to take a railway journey in these days, it must not be forgotten that many of the people living on the Mid-Suffolk line have seldom - and some never - been in a train before. There can be no hesitation in saying that the entire district has been looking forward to the opening with great eagerness, and that practically everybody, even down to the school-children, look upon it as a very great boon to themselves individually, while those who have business associations with the outer world know that it is destined to be an immense advantage to the district.

For the guidance of those innocents who had indeed never been on a train before, and the admonition of high-spirited and anti-social passengers, the Mid-Suffolk company, like all others, had its legal advisers prepare an elaborate set of bye-laws giving it powers to prosecute offenders. Intriguingly these were not in force in time for the start of passenger services, a series of minor omissions from the proofs having exasperated Board of Trade officials empowered to give final approval, so in theory a passenger could have misbehaved in any number of ways during the first week with impunity. The bye-laws were finally approved on 3rd October, taking immediate effect, and from then on the

---

* These were actually the times for departure from Haughley.

company could invoke the rigours of the law against anyone spitting or betting on one of its trains, travelling while drunk or, as a male over the age of eight, attempting to enter a 'Ladies Only' compartment.

There was still one group of people along the line who remained frustratingly unable to benefit from the service now offered: the scattered community between Stradbroke and Laxfield eventually served by the tiny station at Wilby. Such a station had featured in the original plans for the line, but the company had concluded that it would generate little traffic and dropped the idea. Once the line opened, a petition from local people produced a change of heart and a short platform and shelter were hurriedly erected, trains calling from August 1909 although the station took another year to figure in *Bradshaw*.

The service available to passengers at the outset consisted of two trains on weekdays in each direction, leaving Laxfield at 7.35 am and shortly after noon, and departing from Haughley at 10.00 am and 3.30 pm; it was not long before these were augmented. Initially, it appears, freight and passenger operations were kept largely separate, although mixed trains - the opening service was officially described as such - soon became a regular feature, requiring longer journey times. (The fastest ever scheduled passenger-only service between Haughley and Laxfield took just 62 minutes for the 19 miles; mixed trains could take a good half-hour longer.) The commencement of passenger as well as freight services also put a strain on the company's limited motive power, and a third tank engine was ordered from Hudswell, Clarke who had apparently recovered their faith in the Mid-Suffolk's credit-worthiness. Until it could be delivered, saddle tanks named *Emlyn* and, later, *Chamberlain* were hired to provide cover.

One difficulty the line faced in attracting passengers, and retaining them once competition from bus services and the private car began to develop, was the distance of many villages from the stations purporting to serve them. Only Mendlesham and, to a lesser extent Stradbroke, Laxfield and Worlingworth had a station conveniently sited, and the railway lacked the 'pull' ever to encourage residential development close to its stopping points. The Mid-Suffolk company recognised the problem at the outset, and made sure passengers knew how to get to or from the villages. Conveyances (most of them traps) met passengers at each station and took them to their final destinations. Each village had its own trap, and details were printed on the company's timetable handbills.

Compared to the fares of today, the sums charged by the Mid-Suffolk to travel on its trains appear as 'trifling' as the chronicler of the opening suggested. Yet given the distance the line covered and the wages and prices of the day in a hard working farming society where there was little cash to spare, they could add up. Third class fares were exactly one old penny per mile and first class in the region of 2*d*., tickets for both classes being printed on pink card. While the lowest third class fares from Haughley, 4½*d*. to Mendlesham, and from Laxfield, to Wilby once open for 2½*d*., might seem little enough, a third-class single from Laxfield to Haughley or vice versa would cost 1*s*. 7*d*., and a return 3*s*. 2*d*. The highest fare quoted solely for the Mid-Suffolk was a period return first class over the entire line, which cost 5*s*. 3*d*. Third class cheap returns were available on Ipswich market day (Tuesday) to Haughley by the first up train for 1½ times the single fare (2s. 4½d.); on Saturdays returns at 1¼ times the single fare were issued for return no later than the following Monday. When Sunday services were briefly operated, cheap returns could be obtained to any station on the line for a minimum 6d., for return that day or the next. For children aged between three and eleven inclusive, half-fares were charged, with fractions of 1d. on day returns counting as 1d. As far as bookings beyond the line from Mid-Suffolk stations were concerned, these were normally offered to Stowmarket, Ipswich and Liverpool Street.

The line's published receipts for its first full month of operation, October 1908, give an intriguing picture of where the business was coming from, with Laxfield scoring surprisingly heavily compared with larger centres *en route*, presumably because of its function as a railhead. The combined receipts for passengers and freight (with smaller stations and depots such as Gipping, Brockford and Horham included with their nearest neighbours) were:

	£	s.	d.	% of total
Haughley	57	15	0	25
Mendlesham	22	16	0	10
Aspall	18	17	8	9
Kenton	18	7	2	8
Stradbroke	34	10	7	14
Laxfield	79	7	8	34
	£231	14	1	

With the line, or at least the Haughley-Laxfield section of it, now open to all traffic, the staff had reached its peak of just over 60. The somewhat top heavy management had been reduced as the ambitions of the company subsided and funds became tight, but with the commencement of passenger services every station had to be fully staffed instead of, as previously, only having someone on duty when a goods train was being dealt with. Every station was staffed by one 'signal porter' except for Stradbroke, where there was also a station master. Eventually that station took over from Laxfield as the accounting centre for the line, the clerical staff transferring there.

The staff might have been expected to be even larger, given the number of level crossings which from the outset was a feature of the line that attracted notice in the world beyond. However, of the 114 crossings between Haughley and Laxfield, only seven required paid crossing keepers. (Had the line been completed, the number of crossings would have been considerably higher, though not proportionately so as the terrain on the sections left unfinished was considerably more hilly.) At the beginning few of the crossings were gated, the vast majority being 'occupation' crossings used for their own purposes by farmers and the like, but this informal regime came to an abrupt end after a fatal accident at Mendlesham in April 1910.

It was 4.33 on a Friday afternoon when Mrs Laura Wightman, the elderly and unfortunately deaf wife of the village vet and farrier, stepped onto the Atkin's Farm crossing on her way home with a can of milk. She was struck and killed by the afternoon train from Laxfield, comprising one of the Hudswell, Clarke tank engines travelling bunker first, two carriages and four vans. Driver A.

Laxfield station in its earliest days recalled in a collection of local memorabilia. Locomotive No. 3 has just arrived with a train from Haughley.

Stradbroke station photographed about 1909 with locomotive No. 3 arriving with a goods train from Laxfield. Note the open wagon converted to box wagon, second from the locomotive.

L&GRP

Boag had slowed to around 9 mph for the crossing and whistled three times, but to no avail; Mrs Wightman kept walking 'very slowly' onto the track and looking straight ahead. Mr Boag pulled the engine up 65 yards beyond the point where Mrs Wightman was struck and the train crew plus several staff travelling in the guard's van hurried to give first aid, but the inquest at Mendlesham the following week was told she had died instantly from a broken neck. The East Suffolk coroner, Mr L.H. Valliamy, said he was satisfied the driver did all in his power to avoid the accident, and the jury returned a verdict of 'Accidental Death'.

Commenting on the case, the *East Anglian Daily Times* noted that 'the crossing at which the accident occurred has always been thought by the residents to be extremely dangerous, having no gates and sometimes being a playground for the children'. The Mid-Suffolk company, on whose behalf Mr Gillingwater had expressed condolences to the victim's husband at the inquest, reacted promptly by installing gates on the busiest crossings which had thus far been denied them; once the work was complete there were 31 full, gated level crossings, and another 12 with cattle grids, the approach to which required trains to slow to 10 mph. Apart from the small number of crossings remote and busy enough to have their own keepers, a further 11 lay adjacent to stations, with the staff there opening and closing them as necessary. The gating and staffing of crossings was not, however, necessarily a guarantee of safety; in December 1911 a train unable to stop on icy rails smashed through one of the gates of Brockford crossing before the keeper could get it open.

The classification of the line as a 'light railway' also meant that the level crossings did not each have to be protected by signals; indeed there were only four signals over the entire course of the line and nothing that would pass as a signal box. The signals, and the points on running lines, were worked from ground frames, the signals being wired to the points. The signals, all of them lower-quadrant homes protecting stations, were on the approaches to Haughley (MSLR) (when trains moved to the GER station they were governed also by main line signals), Kenton (from both directions) and on the western approach to Laxfield.

Within days of the passenger service commencing, the Mid-Suffolk company effectively conceded that the Kenton-Westerfield branch would never be completed. The rails on the Debenham section were already rusting away, and the management now moved to raise urgently-needed cash by selling for £3,150 to a Stoke-on-Trent firm the stock of new rail it had purchased for the rest of the branch. This was the nearest the company ever came to a formal decision to abandon the scheme, much of the track already laid remaining in place until 1916.

The company still had hopes of reaching Halesworth, however, and in May 1909 a formal application was made to the Commissioners for yet another variation of route, the *Halesworth Advertiser* reporting great local satisfaction that completion of the railway was once again in prospect. It turned out that the Mid-Suffolk's proposals for entering the town over the Southwold's right of way had been quietly rejected at the height of the company's financial crisis. Furthermore, Major Daniel and his advisers had concluded that the only practicable way of effecting a junction with the GER at Halesworth was to revert to the northern

MSLR locomotive No. 3 (before it gained a sandbox on its buffer beam) seen next to a wayside siding - probably Brown Street - on its way up the line with a freight train from Haughley.

Ken Nunn Collection

Locomotive No. 3 waiting for the 'Right Away' from Haughley (MSLR) station with a mixed train during the later years of independent operation. *L&GRP*

route approved in 1903, which had been abandoned as too ambitious with work already in hand. The company thus sought a third Amendment Order not only reviving its powers to build the line along that route, but also to reactivate its rights to compulsory purchase which would shortly lapse.

The officials required to make a recommendation to the then President of the Board of Trade, Mr Winston Churchill, were not this time concerned about the feasibility of the route or the objections to it raised at the hearing six years before. Their doubts were technical: was there any precedent for the approval of fresh works by a railway company in receivership which had yet to reach agreement with its creditors? The Inland Revenue, with pride of place among those still hoping to recover what was owed them, signalled that it had no objection and Mr Churchill was recommended to make one of the less significant decisions of his political career. The Amendment Order approving once again the construction of the northern route to Halesworth was duly granted on 9th December, 1909, but the project was stillborn, the company's finances precluding any attempt to start work, and the powers to complete the line lapsed in 1912. The LNER's records give the date as 1911, but that may refer to the powers to construct the section from Cratfield to the start of the deviation east of Huntingfield, which had been renewed earlier. In any event, the Mid-Suffolk company was never again to indicate publicly that it was still aiming for completion, even though as late as 1921 it would be stated that £94,106 out of the maximum £300,000 to be spent on the promotion and construction of the line had never been called upon.

Where the running of trains was concerned, the Mid-Suffolk management was proving rather more adventurous. It was not long before the basic two trains each way per day were augmented by a third passenger working from Kenton to Haughley and back, starting from Laxfield on Saturdays only. By the timetable of April 1910 the following passenger and mixed trains (plus some unlisted workings for freight only) were running:

	8.25	am	ex-Laxfield	arr. Haughley	9.32	am
SO	11.35	am	ex-Laxfield	arr. Haughley	12.42	pm
SX	12.00	noon	ex-Kenton	arr. Haughley	12.42	pm
SX	3.35	pm	ex-Laxfield	arr. Haughley	4.52	pm
SO	3.45	pm	ex-Laxfield	arr. Haughley	4.52	pm
	10.00	am	ex-Haughley	arr. Laxfield	11.02	am
SO	2.32	pm	ex-Haughley	arr. Laxfield	3.39	pm
SX	2.37	pm	ex-Haughley	arr. Kenton	3.30	pm
TuO	5.40	pm	ex-Haughley	arr. Laxfield	6.45	pm
TuX	5.55	pm	ex-Haughley	arr. Laxfield	7.00	pm

Passengers from Laxfield by the early morning train could reach Liverpool Street at 12.27 pm (in 4 hours 2 minutes) and have almost three hours in London before the last connecting train back, which left at 3.20 pm. The Tuesdays-only 5.40 pm from Haughley was timed to connect with a market 'special' from Ipswich. By implication the trains which normally ran as 'mixed' were the weekday return working between Kenton and Haughley, which may have carried freight over the rest of the line though its locomotive was stabled at Kenton, and the 3.35 from Laxfield on Mondays to Fridays, with slightly more generous timings than its Saturday counterpart.

The pattern of services remained fluid and the summer of 1911 saw further changes, with the introduction of a Sunday service of two trains a day each way, the first being early enough to discourage all but the most determined of day excursionists. The full service of passenger and mixed trains was:

Weekdays

MO	6.40	am	ex-Laxfield	*arr.* Haughley	7.47	am
MX	8.20	am	ex-Laxfield	*arr.* Haughley	9.27	am
TuFO	12.10	pm	ex-Kenton	*arr.* Haughley	12.52	pm
MSO	12.00	noon	ex-Laxfield	*arr.* Haughley	1.14	pm
	3.20	pm	ex-Laxfield	*arr.* Haughley	4.37	pm
	10.00	am	ex-Haughley	*arr.* Laxfield	11.02	am
SX	2.37	pm	ex-Haughley	*arr.* Kenton	3.25	pm
SO	3.00	pm	ex-Haughley	*arr.* Laxfield	4.29	pm
	5.55	pm	ex-Haughley	*arr.* Laxfield	7.00	pm

Sundays

7.00	am	ex-Laxfield	*arr.* Haughley	8.07	am
5.17	pm	ex-Laxfield	*arr.* Haughley	6.27	pm
8.50	am	ex-Haughley	*arr.* Laxfield	9.52	am
7.35	pm	ex-Haughley	*arr.* Laxfield	8.37	pm

The Sunday service aside, the main feature of the timetable was the disappearance of any midday train toward Haughley on Wednesdays and Thursdays. In all probability, given the existence of a working the other way, it ran but carried freight only.

By October 1911 the Sunday service had gone, for the winter at least. The 2.37 pm Haughley-Kenton ran each weekday (Laxfield thus losing its third incoming service on Saturdays), and the 5.55 pm from Haughley reverted on Tuesdays to a 5.40 departure to suit market day passengers from Ipswich.

The up service was also revised. The first train now left Laxfield at 8.20 am every weekday - surely a necessity for school children - and that village also lost its midday train on Mondays and Saturdays; the noon service from Kenton to Haughley now ran every weekday, restoring the Wednesday and Thursday workings. The changes may well have been brought about by a decision to speed up the passenger service and operate freight traffic separately wherever possible because of the amount of time taken up by shunting: to keep this to a minimum, mixed trains leaving Haughley were marshalled with goods wagons at the rear in the order they were to be detached; at each station the entire train was reversed until the wagons bound for it were in the siding. Indeed one feature of the timetable was the offering of what could have been the fastest ever timing between Liverpool Street and Laxfield: 3 hours 25 minutes by the 3.20 pm departure from the London terminus. The up journey was less spectacular: 4 hours 7 minutes for the 102 miles.

Chapter Four

The Line Described

Haughley to Kenton

There was an important railway junction at Haughley long before a line branched off into Mid-Suffolk territory, and there is one there today, though the sizeable station that accompanied it has gone. Indeed, ironically, all of the four Great Eastern stations where a junction was originally planned by the Mid-Suffolk remain in use save for the one the line actually reached. Haughley itself is only a small place, with a population of perhaps 200, atop a hill on what was once the main road from Ipswich and Stowmarket to Bury St Edmunds, and the siting of its station three-quarters of a mile away at the foot of the hill was a clear enough sign that the village was not a railway objective in itself; indeed between 1866 and 1890 the station was known officially as Haughley Road. The lane from Haughley was dominated until World War II by a windmill erected for its owner by a company of soldiers who were conveniently passing *en route* to Harwich to join Wellington's army in the Peninsular War against Napoleon.

The railway arrived at Haughley on Christmas Eve, 1846, when the Ipswich and Bury company's line between Suffolk's two county towns was opened, initially to freight traffic alone. A week later the Ipswich and Bury amalgamated with the Eastern Union Railway, which ran from Colchester to Ipswich. Haughley became a junction on 7th June, 1848, when the Eastern Union opened the first section of its line from there to Norwich as far as Finningham; this required the closure of the original Haughley station, a mile along what now became the Bury branch, during 1849 after the shortest of lives, and its re-siting at the junction. The new main line reached Burston on 2nd July that year and Norwich on 7th November. The Eastern Union was absorbed into the Great Eastern Railway on its incorporation on 1st August, 1862, and that company's ambition of a main line terminus at Liverpool Street was fulfilled after more than its fair share of setbacks on 1st November, 1875.

Haughley GER station (frequently described as 'Haughley Junction') was 83 miles from Liverpool Street, 14¼ from Ipswich and 2¼ from Stowmarket, the nearest town of any size and next station to the south. By the first line built through Haughley, it was 12¼ miles to Bury St Edmunds and, by routes diverging just short of Newmarket, 40¼ miles to Ely and 41¼ to Cambridge. On the main line into Norfolk, Diss (now the only intermediate station open) was 12 miles away and Norwich itself 32 miles distant.

While the Bury line has always been rated the lesser of the two, each of the routes joining at Haughley was then and remains of considerable importance. The Norwich line was developed by the Great Eastern with express services from Liverpool Street not only to the cathedral city but to the resorts beyond, notably Cromer. It also carried its fair share of local and agricultural traffic and long-distance freight. The Bury route carried cross-country services (via Ely) bringing passengers from the Midlands and North to the Essex resorts and the ferries which

Haughley (GER) station very soon after the opening of the Mid-Suffolk Light Railway to freight traffic. Note the MSLR wagon in the siding, and also the unamended station nameboard.

Lens of Sutton

Haughley (GER) station from the east; the MSLR station was reached by the ramp on the right. Today only the room at the extreme left of this picture is still standing. *Lens of Sutton*

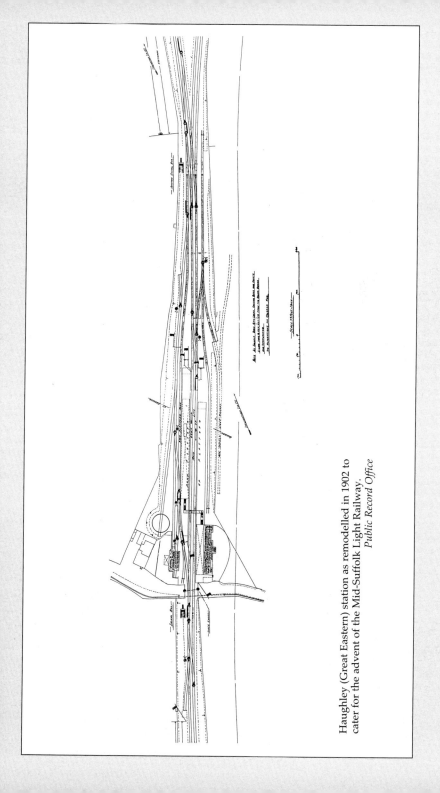

Haughley (Great Eastern) station as remodelled in 1902 to
cater for the advent of the Mid-Suffolk Light Railway.
Public Record Office

No. 65447 on arrival at Haughley with the 1.45 pm from Laxfield in September 1951. The 6-wheel carriages are just weeks away from the scrapyard. Note the brake van - the only freight presence on a supposedly 'mixed' train - and the young helper on the footplate. The open doors betray the fact that on this occasion the 1.45 actually carried some passengers.   *H.C. Casserley*

Haughley (GER) station seen here from the south in its later days. The awning has been removed from the footbridge and the nameboard is now a standard British Railways issue. By this time the 'Middy' had closed, but tracks still remained in the grain sidings.   *Lens of Sutton*

Haughley (GER) station seen here from the south, appearing as it did for most of its life. The points on the level crossing led to the west side of the island platform. An Ipswich train is signalled.
Lens of Sutton

No. 65447 lurks behind the imposing station nameboard at Haughley in between duties on the Mid-Suffolk. Its train is out of camera-shot to the left.

No. 65447 in the bay at Haughley with a mixed train for Laxfield; the bogie carriages pinpoint the period as the last few months of the line's existence.
Lens of Sutton

the Great Eastern operated to the Continent from Harwich. It also bore a sizeable freight traffic, both to and from Felixstowe, Harwich and Ipswich docks and in the form of coal from the Midlands. Equally it formed a useful outlet for East Suffolk's farm produce. Haughley itself enjoyed regular local passenger services on both routes, with some semi-fast trains to Norwich also calling. Even more important for its role as a junction, it became - and was to remain until well into the 1960s - the crossing point for the night mail trains between Liverpool Street, Ipswich and Peterborough, from which connecting services ran to Norwich.

While passenger and freight traffic originating from Haughley were never heavy, a sizeable station and complicated trackwork were needed to handle its workings as a junction. The lines to Norwich and Bury, each double track, diverged just north of the station. The station house and main buildings, in a style familiar throughout central Suffolk, were on the up platform which was covered by a curved awning. A footbridge, also covered for most of the station's life, led to the island down platform, which was staggered slightly to the north and could boast a canopy but only minimal buildings. The loop line serving the western face of that platform reached only the Bury route, crossovers beyond the confines of the station enabling trains in either direction to use it. This track rejoined the down main line on the level crossing immediately south of the station, the roadway of which led to Haughley village and was eventually named Station Road. The loop line outlet was protected by catch points, and there were instances of trains arriving from Bury overshooting the platform and crashing through the fence into Station Road. The most dramatic of these, during World War II, involved a train scattering its load of bombs, one of which lodged under the firebox of the locomotive with a fireman playing his hose on it to prevent an explosion which could have wrecked the entire station. From the loop line two sidings, one long and one a mere stub, ran into a goods bay, and a further one of medium length ended in a turntable, which disappeared well before the end. At the outset Haughley (GER) could boast two signal boxes, one by the crossing and the other where the main routes diverged north of the station; the box at the crossing, governing the station and the approach to it from the MSLR, was eliminated in 1932 when the light railway's sole signal also came under the control of the remaining box at the junction.

Haughley station in Great Eastern days was a busy place with a sizeable staff and, not surprisingly, its fair share of characters. George Ewart Evans in *Where Beards Wag All*, his delightful book on life in this part of Suffolk, told of how one of the porters dozed off in church and, when roused, leapt to his feet crying: 'Haughley, Haughley, change for Finningham, Mellis and all stations to Norwich!' It would have been the most frequent call he had to make, as while the Norwich line was the 'main' one, most of the trains stopping at Haughley were bound for Bury. Nevertheless the station nameboards read: 'Haughley Junction, for Bury, Newmarket and Cambridge branch'. To this was later added: 'For Mid-Suffolk Light Railway'.

The advent of the Mid-Suffolk brought changes, most of them on the up side. A siding for transferred goods wagons from the MSLR was constructed beside the station, though at first without a platform face, and to the north was installed a headshunt served by trailing connections from both the up main line and the

Mid-Suffolk terminus. This was a temporary arrangement; the MSLR was eager to use the Great Eastern station when full services began. However the main line company first claimed that this would require wholesale remodelling and then quoted charges way beyond the means of an already-struggling undertaking, so the MSLR's Directors ordered the construction of a separate station.

That station lay adjacent to the Great Eastern's and slightly to the north. Its modest office building, standard MSLR design for its 'large' stations, was not quite what it seemed, the apparently sturdy brick edifice proving on closer examination to be a wooden frame covered in brick-patterned zinc sheet, resembling a station in an old-style clockwork train set. (All other Mid-Suffolk station buildings were of pitch pine, save for one of the buildings at Laxfield which was the Haughley station's 'twin'.) The building stood on a single gravelled platform on the east side of the terminal track, which had a run-round loop from which led a spur to the Great Eastern headshunt and two sidings. The platform line and loop terminated at the south end in parallel spurs, between which was a staithe. Close by was the water supply for the Mid-Suffolk locomotives, lifted to tank level by a petrol-powered beam engine; after the grouping the GER supply was used. One notable omission was the cattle pen which was a feature of every other Mid-Suffolk station; as all cattle passing through Haughley were reckoned to be shipped straight out over the Great Eastern, there was felt to be no need - though inevitably some local traffic did have to be accommodated, the beasts being loaded from the Great Eastern staithe to the west of the island platform.

When a Mid-Suffolk train arrived, passengers transferring to Great Eastern trains had to walk the hundred yards or so to the main line station, to wait for their local connections as expresses hauled by 'Claud Hamiltons' pounded through. (The covered ways predicted by Mr Stevenson for passengers changing at Westerfield and Halesworth were never in the plans for Haughley.) Milk churns, parcels, poultry and other 'small consignments' were hurriedly transferred to the GER station by barrow for onward shipment, the Haughley station staff gaining considerable exercise. While this process was under way the train crew would refill the tanks, uncouple goods wagons and cattle trucks from the rear of the train and propel them onto the single exchange siding, which was eventually supplemented.

After the Grouping, the Great Eastern and Mid-Suffolk stations became known as Haughley (West) and (East) respectively. In due course, the LNER decided to economise by running Mid-Suffolk trains from the main station, and constructed a bay platform on the up side to make this possible, with a run-round loop added to the siding already in place. The MSLR signal for entry to the terminus - a long-stemmed Home with a shunting disc half way up - was removed at the same time as the track into the East station, movements by then being signalled from the Haughley Junction box with an LNER home signal some way up Haughley Bank covering the approach to the junction.

As the transfer of Mid-Suffolk trains to the main station took place in November 1939 and the MSLR station was immediately flattened to make way for extra exchange sidings, it was probably hastened by the onset of war; only minor strengthening to the exchange sidings had been carried out after the outbreak of World War I. The demands of munitions and trooping traffic, and the opening there of an asphalt plant for airfield construction, brought added

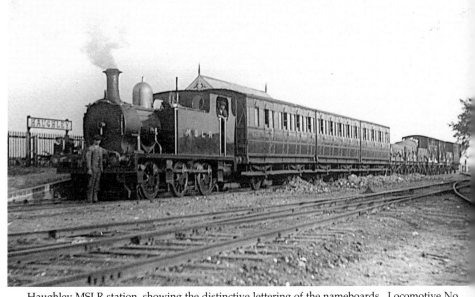

Haughley MSLR station, showing the distinctive lettering of the nameboards. Locomotive No. 3 prepares to leave with a mixed train. The connection to the GER can be seen on the far right of the photograph.   *Ken Nunn Collection*

A 'Blackwall Tank', No. 7247 seen here arriving at Haughley East station in 1932, with a lengthy mixed train.   *Dr Ian C. Allen*

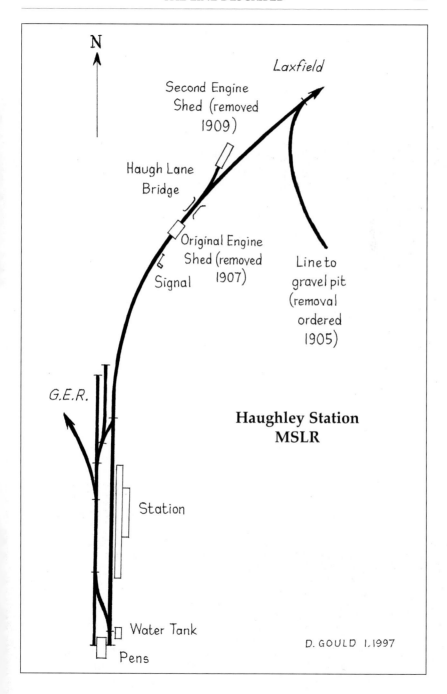

N

Laxfield

Second Engine
Shed (removed
1909)

Haugh Lane
Bridge

Original Engine
Shed (removed
Signal   1907)

Line to
gravel pit
(removal
ordered
1905)

G.E.R.

**Haughley Station
MSLR**

Station

Water Tank

D. GOULD 1.1997

Pens

importance and congestion to Haughley, and in the process of remodelling the tracks were rearranged in a way that for the first time permitted through running off the main line to Laxfield; the excursion to Felixstowe on the second day of passenger operation, and all subsequent such bargain trips, apparently involved a change of train at Haughley. In practice the new facility enabled one Mid-Suffolk train a day to start back from Stowmarket, with pupils for stations on the branch from that town's County Grammar and Secondary Modern schools. (While trains *from* Laxfield could have run into Haughley station and on to Stowmarket without any reversing, none was ever diagrammed to do so.) On arrival at Haughley the train for Laxfield ran through the station, then set back into the up platform to gain access to the branch. On its run up the bank from Stowmarket it had followed immediately behind a Norwich express; for a few brief months in 1951/52 this brought within minutes the contrasting sight of a brand new 'Britannia' Pacific at full pelt with a train of main line stock, followed by a 'J15' 0-6-0 of advancing years hauling at first three GER six-wheelers of almost equal age, and then two redundant bogie carriages from East London suburban services.

In 1950 came a spectacular change to a stationscape which had remained essentially the same for a century: construction by the Government of a multi-storey grain dryer on the site of the Mid-Suffolk station, served by several long sidings. Still a landmark for miles around, the building won unexpected praise from Dr Nikolaus Pevsner in the Suffolk volume of his *The Buildings of England*. He described the dryer, designed by A. Swift for the Ministry of Works, as 'an excellent, "anonymous", piece of recent industrial architecture, and just because it is so at ease it goes perfectly well with the nature around'. The sidings outlasted the line to Laxfield, being relaid after its closure before eventually succumbing to the shift of agricultural traffic to the roads; the bay platform was removed in 1960.

The first landmark on the Mid-Suffolk line as it curved sharply eastward to climb out of Haughley was the original engine shed for the terminus. Provided in the first instance to house one of the contractor's two Manning, Wardle locomotives, this structure astonishingly straddled the running line. Lt-Col von Donop was profoundly unimpressed by this arrangement when he inspected the line in 1905, and he ordered the shed's removal, but photographs show it still there two years later. For a short time after its demolition, a locomotive was housed instead in a shed on a short spur just beyond Haugh Lane bridge - but this, too, was under sentence from the Board of Trade and stabling of engines at Haughley had ended by 1909, Kenton taking over the duty.

Trains from the Mid-Suffolk station, and later from the junction itself, passed over Haugh Lane bridge - one of three carrying railways over the same minor road in the space of 100 yards - as soon as they left the confines of Haughley yard. The bridge's construction was faulty and had to be repaired in 1905, and showed further signs of weakness when surveyed in 1933; when the exchange sidings were relaid at the start of the war, it was given a new and stronger deck. The opportunity was also taken then to re-lay the first few hundred yards of the Mid-Suffolk with a heavier rail, as it had come within the limit of shunt and main line locomotives needed to set back onto it, tender engines thus appearing on the branch for the first time. No corresponding improvements were made to the signalling, and Mid-Suffolk trains approaching down Haughley Bank were put under orders to proceed with caution in case shunting was in progress - hardly a ruling to inspire confidence.

By the time it passed over Haugh Lane bridge, the Mid-Suffolk line was not only curving sharply but beginning a steep climb. Haughley Bank confronted trains with a pull of just over half a mile at 1 in 50 (sometimes cited as 1 in 42) followed by a further short stretch at 1 in 88. This climb, which had to be attacked from a standing start, was the greatest obstacle to train operation on the entire line, with the risk of a runaway on the downgrade ploughing into the terminus, or, later, blocking the main line, potentially a greater danger than the inability of a train to struggle to the summit. This was recognised by the imposition of a special limit of 14 wagons on down trains as far as Gipping, the first stop for most of the line's working life, and 21 in the other direction. As an additional safety measure on downward journeys, the early Tuesday cattle train for Ipswich market was divided at Gipping, the rear portion waiting with brakes pinned on until the engine could return for it.

Neither the MSLR's own locomotives nor the GER's 'Blackwall Tanks' which succeeded them were ever entirely free from trouble on this climb, as even a full head of steam at the start would not guarantee a successful ascent. Both types of engine could stall, but the Mid-Suffolk tanks were often able to blow off and restart, while their heavier Great Eastern counterparts tended to slip, and frequently had to return to the junction and attack the gradient again. The 'Blackwall Tanks' were brought in after an LNER locomotive inspector's embarrassing experience with the line's original locomotives when he tried them on Haughley Bank immediately after the Grouping. The technique used by the line's own drivers to get their charges up the bank offended his professional sensibilities, and he determined to show them how it should be done. To the locals' delight he failed in several attempts to get a test train up the bank and retired in high dudgeon.

In the line's earliest years, train operations on Haughley Bank were complicated by a set of trailing points half way up, from which a 240-yard spur ran to the gravel pits that had produced much of the ballast for the line. The pits were almost worked out during 1903 but the points were still there two years later when the Board of Trade ordered their removal.

From this junction, close to which the LNER erected its own home signal to replace that of the MSLR, the line climbed to Silver Street crossing, the highest point on the 'Middy' at 214 ft. It then fell away at 1 in 50 to the Stowmarket-Finningham Road, where there was a further gated crossing (original plans for a bridge having been dropped). Just before the crossing after that, Brown Street, there was during the line's construction a contractor's siding complete with water tank. This, rather than Gipping, was probably the location of the 'Old Newton' station that figured in the original plans for the line; Brown Street siding was the closest point on the line to the small village of that name, which was also that distance from Haughley station. It was at the Brown Street crossing in the late 1940s that an unwary male pedestrian was run down by a train, one of only two known fatalities in the history of the line. Not long after a car carrying an elderly couple was impaled on the front of a class 'J15' 0-6-0

Coasting into Haughley MSLR (at the foot of the bank), No. 3 is signalled into the terminus. The home signal covered the station and the shunting disc beneath it the loop line.

Ken Nunn Collection

Locomotive No. 3 attacks Haughley Bank with a mixed train, which is just passing over Haugh Lane road bridge. By the time this picture was taken in 1909, the engine shed over the running line (*shown on p. 24*) just beyond the bridge had gone.

Ken Nunn Collection

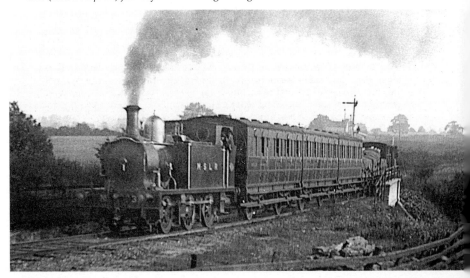

edging round the blind curve from Haughley. From there trains passed along a short but substantial embankment to reach Gipping.

Gipping (2 miles)

This stopping place was probably never intended to handle passengers as well as freight. Three-quarters of a mile from the hamlet of Gipping and a considerable distance further from Old Newton, it could have expected to attract passengers only from the handful of farms and cottages nearby. Little more than a loop with headshunt and a hut at the end of a farm lane, Gipping siding contributed little to traffic. Not ready for the opening of the line to goods traffic in September 1904, it eventually settled down to an unspectacular career handling occasional truck and van loads of farm produce and supplies. Its main use in later years was to house wagons for which there was no space in Haughley yard - plus in wartime the occasional ammunition truck bound for Mendlesham. After the elimination of Brown Street siding, Gipping also justified its existence as the point where wagons on trains too heavy to traverse Haughley Bank in their entirety could be left until the locomotive could return for them.

From Gipping, where there was a further level crossing, the line continued east-north-east across open fields and over four more country lanes in the direction of Mendlesham. It was on this stretch around 1920 that an incident occurred which demonstrated both the remoteness of the line and the resourcefulness of the company's staff. Mr Geoff Rice, a local expert on the line in early days, recalled* that it took place when the last train of the day from Haughley, with driver Cliff Bloom and foreman Charlie Brunning on the footplate, was picking up speed after surmounting the bank:

The fireman opened the fire door to inspect the fire, whereupon it was promptly blown out into the cab in a blast of steam, filling the cab with red hot coals, steam and smoke. The engine had burst a tube. The train was stranded midway between Haughley and Mendlesham and the crew knew that at that time of day the nearest relief was at the other end of the line at Laxfield. The other two locomotives were shedded for the night, the fires were dropped and the crews had gone home. More passengers than usual were on the mixed train that evening as an excursion had been booked from the line that day. Special plugs were included in the tool kit for this eventuality but they would not serve. Finally the crew sharpened the end of a shunter's pole and drove a piece into each end of the damaged tube with the coal hammer. The end burned off when the fire was raised but enough remained to block the tube. The plugs leaked and the smokebox door had to be left ajar to prevent the water rising in the smokebox. Steam was raised, and in this state the train limped into Mendlesham. Laxfield was telephoned and the standby engine requested. The crew decided to attempt to make their way to the crossing place, Kenton. They lightened the train by leaving the goods trucks at Mendlesham and then struggled on to Kenton where the relief engine was waiting to take over.

Now travelling due east and still across almost flat country, the line now reached Mendlesham.

* For the Ipswich and District Historical Society's 1967/68 handbook.

Mendlesham station manages to look busy as a train for Laxfield pauses there in 1951.

H.C. Casserley

A close-up from 1951 of the distinctive MSLR station nameboard at Mendlesham, showing the company's unique style of lettering. Note also that the uprights are two sections of rail.

H.C. Casserley

Mendlesham station seen from the west; note two-bay construction of the building - now at Brockford - and the diminutive 'Gents'. Appearances can be deceptive; this was one of the line's busier stations.

Lens of Sutton

Mendlesham (4½ miles)

This was the largest community directly served by the line, with a population fractionally under 1,000 during most of its lifetime, a couple of score ahead of Stradbroke. The Mid-Suffolk station was also well sited for this former market town, whose church is described by Pevsner as having 'urban pretensions'. But the village was close enough to the main Ipswich-Norwich road for its traffic to become vulnerable to bus competition. The station was just south of the village, immediately before a level crossing taking what is now 'Old Station Road' on to the smaller village of Mendlesham Green, a mile and a half further south.

On the Haughley side of the station was a siding running parallel with the through track to its north, with a short spur. This proved inadequate to cope with the extra wartime traffic for the Mendlesham air base, some wagons having to wait their turn at Gipping - a relief to the villagers as they were often carrying high explosive. The buffers of the spur abutted the ramp of the platform, also on the down side, with a corrugated iron and timber building of standard MSLR design (two bays, with a tiny canopy, and a flat-roofed toilet adjoining it); this building, beside which during the war the occasional bemused American airman waited to go on leave, has survived and now adorns the platform of the reconstructed Brockford station. Nameboards were in the company's unique spindly, almost *art nouveau*, style.

Most trains were timed to do the 4½ miles from Haughley to Mendlesham, the first passenger station, in 12 minutes, a stiff timing given the hurdle of Haughley Bank. Furthermore the 25 mph limit on the line - 10 mph at ungated crossings with cattle grids - made it all the harder to recover lost time, assuming it was observed. It was at a then ungated crossing close to Mendlesham, it should be recalled, that Mrs Wightman the village vet's wife met an untimely end in 1909 when a train ran her down.

Now on a downgrade, the line left the station over a level crossing and headed for Mendlesham Ford, some 300 yards on at the south-eastern extremity of the village. Here was an instance of the contractor's habit of overruling the Mid-Suffolk Board on how the line should be constructed. The plans provided for a bridge over the road there, but as the target date for opening neared and Jackson's did nothing to provide it, a level crossing had to be substituted. Omission of the bridge meant that the line had to fall away from Mendlesham station at 1 in 50, instead of starting its descent after the road had been crossed.

In its very early days, the line also crossed the main A140 Ipswich-Norwich road on the level, just over a mile beyond Mendlesham station. One charitably imagines that this was a temporary right of way, and that the contractor was not seeking to avoid construction of what in the event was one of only two underbridges completed. Freight trains used these contractor's metals during the first ten months of operation from September 1904, until work was complete on a cutting 20 ft deep and nearly 500 yards in length to enable the main road to bridge the railway by means of a brick-and-girder construction; the 1 in 50 downgrade continued until the bridge was reached, after which trains had to contend with a similar uphill gradient. Just under half a mile beyond this substantial piece of civil engineering for a minor line, the first of the smaller passenger stations was reached: Brockford and Wetheringsett.

A ganger's trolley at Brockford station in the days before relaying of the track in 1934. The gangers poles appear to be located over crankpins on the wheels of the trolley to provide propulsion. *R.M. Casserley Collection*

Brockford seen here in the line's final months, looking towards Haughley. Neither the LNER nor British Railways ever tried to impose their style on the MSLR's wayside stations. Compare this view with the re-constructed Brockford station on page 4. *R.M. Casserley*

Brockford and Wetheringsett (6 miles)

This station, as recreated in slightly different form, is now the focal point of the efforts being made to preserve and hopefully reconstruct a section of the 'Middy', yet it played an unspectacular part in the original line's existence. Simply described on the station nameboards as Brockford, the village adjacent to the station though actually the smaller of the two, it was a mile and a half and four minutes' journey, from Mendlesham. It stood just beyond a level crossing for the road between Wetheringsett, Brockford, Mickfield and Stonham Aspall - a crossing whose gates, despite its proximity to a manned station, were rammed on a number of occasions by trains arriving from Haughley. The gates had to be twice replaced between 1909 and 1911 alone, while in LNER days and later, shattered crossing gates tied together with rope did not prevent the station winning several 'Best Kept' awards. Once again the platform was on the down side, this time with the short siding and spur adjoining it at the Laxfield end, shunting requiring particular skill as the course of the line falls away from the station on a 1 in 50 gradient; because of the track layout, shunting could only be carried out by the locomotive of a down train. In Mid-Suffolk days the siding also housed a petrol-driven trolley for a nine-man permanent way gang who were based there. The original station buildings were considerably smaller than even at Mendlesham: two wooden sheds with corrugated iron roofs, one facing out onto the platform from behind it and comprising a waiting shelter and telephone booth, and the other on the platform itself, sideways-on to the train; one of the two survived the years between closure and revival and stands again on the present platform at Brockford, constructed by enlarging the cattle dock. Opened after the commencement of goods traffic, the station was lightly used, though it did find itself during World War II closer to Mendlesham air base than the station of that name and may have derived some benefit.

Now running almost due east between moated farms of great antiquity, the line made an uneventful progress from Brockford - one reason why this section was chosen for resuscitation - before crossing the B1077 road from Debenham to Eye, to enter Aspall and Thorndon.

Aspall and Thorndon (8½ miles)

This station, which bore only the name 'Aspall', was set in open country and never contributed greatly to passenger traffic; should the revived line ever reach it, its original traffic figures will be dwarfed. The small village of Aspall was a mile away to the south and Thorndon, with a population over 500, almost three miles to the north and as close to the station at Brockford (and, almost, to the GER terminus at Eye which in theory competed with the Mid-Suffolk for passengers until 1931). The village the station came closest to serving was Rishangles, half way to Thorndon. The Mid-Suffolk management did recognise that intending passengers would have difficulty reaching or proceeding from Aspall station, and the 'conveyance' connecting with surrounding farms and communities was needed there more than anywhere else. Aspall station was

Aspall and Thorndon station, April 1952, seen from the window of the morning train from Haughley. Once again the title of the station was abbreviated. *H.C. Casserley*

Aspall between trains, showing signs of habitation. The shadows show plenty of wagons in the siding alongside the running line. *Lens of Sutton*

also advertised as 'for Debenham', two miles to the south, but anyone wishing to travel from Debenham to Ipswich by train would take as long just to get to Haughley as to reach Ipswich by bus. Prior to and just after the Grouping, the station had a distinguished regular passenger in the form of the MSLR Director Mr J.B. Chevallier of Aspall Hall who travelled first class every Tuesday to Ipswich market, a 'Directors' saloon' - a composite carriage in which two compartments had been knocked together - being hitched to the train for himself and his friends.

Aspall station was nevertheless surprisingly busy, its relative lack of passenger traffic being offset by plenty of activity on the goods front, as it was the line's central coal depot and, after the closure of the short-lived branch to Debenham, the railhead for that village. The single coal siding with headshunt was on the up side, facing the station platform across the running line; as at Brockford, shunting was normally left for down trains, though the locomotive of an up train could shunt from the main line using a tow rope. The station proper, not even marked on some maps of the area, comprised a smaller version of the building at Mendlesham, with two bays but no canopy over the entrance to the 'booking office', with a hut at one end and a shed at the other. Most trains were allowed seven minutes for the 2½ miles from Brockford.

Running at first slightly south of east across open country with no road crossings, the line swung to the north-east after three-quarters of a mile and approached Kenton Junction.

Kenton Junction (10 miles)

This station, operationally the mid-point of the line, owed its siting to the convergence of the lines from Haughley and Debenham, rather than any centre of population. As with Aspall the location was open to the elements, which must have been bad news in particular for occupants of a train snowed in there some time in the 1930s. Half a mile from the hamlet of Kenton to the south and almost two miles from the larger village of Bedingfield to the north (the station was actually in Bedingfield parish), it was a busier station than its remoteness would have suggested, again largely on the freight side through the proximity of the Eastern Counties Farmers' depot. The generous layout and facilities, however, underlined the reason for its existence - and the title bestowed in Mid-Suffolk days the hopes unfulfilled. The station served as a junction for barely two years and for freight traffic only; the LNER, in a belated acknowledgement of defeat, referred to it simply as 'Kenton', as did the station nameboards.

Trains approaching from Aspall, a mile and a half away and four minutes' journey, passed some 250 yards out the original site of the Kenton engine shed, from the construction of the line until 1912; it also housed a small workshop. The only surviving clue to its somewhat peculiar siting, which owed more to the needs of the contractor than convenience for the station and yard, was a timber-framed water tower just beyond, at the point where the trackbed of the former Debenham branch curved in. Originally the branch joined the main line 200 yards out from the station level crossing, with a passing loop intervening,

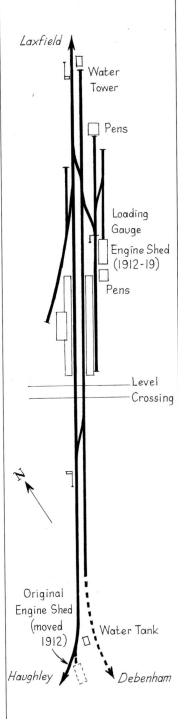

Laxfield

Water Tower

Pens

Loading Gauge

Engine Shed (1912-19)

Pens

Level Crossing

N

Original Engine Shed (moved 1912)

Water Tank

Haughley

Debenham

Left: Track plan of Kenton Junction after closure and lifting of the Debenham branch. At the very beginning the branch joined the 'main' line by the water tower and there was a passing loop between there and the level crossing. The station layout is shown as modified after the adverse Board of Trade report of 1905.

Below: A mixed train leaving Kenton station for Haughley in 1947, with a just-renumbered class 'J65' 0-6-0T No. 8212.
Dr Ian C. Allen

Looking westwards at Kenton station; the siding beyond the level crossing which had been the start of the Debenham branch is clearly visible. Note the trucks standing in what was effectively a third platform to the left.   *H.C. Casserley*

Kenton station in between trains, showing clearly the yard beyond it. The complicated pointwork was mainly operated from a ground frame; points off the running lines were controlled by levers alongside.   *Lens of Sutton*

but during its brief career it was given an approach of its own to Kenton, running alongside the 'main' line with a trailing crossover just as the road was approached. When the branch was lifted, the final 170 yards were kept as a siding, giving the illusion of a double track approach to the station (the level crossing at its western end was the only double track crossing on the line).

Kenton station was planned as the meeting place of three lines of almost equal importance, not as the only passing place on a route to nowhere. It boasted a passing loop, two platforms (one an island), an engine shed until just after World War I and no fewer than five sidings. The loop, moreover, was protected in each direction by home signals; they were installed in preparation for Kenton becoming a full junction, but the fact that they presented their faces to trains approaching disproves the suggestion sometimes made that they were 'starters'. No junction signals, or indeed any signalling for the Debenham branch, appear ever to have been erected. Signals and points alike on the running lines at Kenton were worked from a ground frame.

Toward the end of the line's existence both signals were essentially ornamental, being out of commission for months on end. On one occasion when the signal at the Haughley end of the station had been jammed for some considerable time, station staff were bewildered when an incoming train halted at it, whistling loudly. The ensuing scenes were witnessed by two eminent enthusiasts, Dr Ian C. Allen and Richard Hardy, then a junior official with the LNER, who was on the footplate. The train was the only one on the line that day, a fact well known to all involved, which heightened the puzzlement of the station staff until they suddenly realised that the driver - George Rowse, a Barnsley man who had previously driven the 2-8-8-2 Garratt on coal trains on Worsborough Bank before transferring to Laxfield - was trying to tell them something. His message was straightforward: there was 'management' on board and he, George Rowse, was not going to take his train through a signal at danger, jammed or not. However before this registered, Mr Hardy overheard a conversation on the platform to the effect that 'this signal had been jammed at danger for months past, and what the hell did George think he was doing to stop at it?' When the penny dropped, someone unearthed a green flag to wave the train in; Dr Allen noted that it must have been the original MSLR issue as, when it was unfurled, most of the material had been eaten or rotted away.

Immediately beyond the crossover was Kenton station, with the exception of Laxfield the most complex on the line. It was originally conceived as an island platform with running lines on either side, enabling cross-platform connections between trains to and from Haughley and Westerfield, but a combination of the adverse Board of Trade report in 1905 and the abandonment of the Debenham branch produced a very different layout; this created the impression that the line east to Laxfield, rather than that to the GER at Haughley, was the more important. On the down side was a platform bearing the station building, a standard Mid-Suffolk edifice with a small canopy. Opposite stood the island platform, bare save for a station nameboard and one gas lamp and in latter years covered by grass. The north face served the up line, and the south face a siding boasting a loading gauge and terminating at buffers by the crossing; as originally planned this would have been the running line for Debenham, but in

Kenton's station buildings from the ramp at the Haughley end of the southern (island) platform; the background of the Eastern Counties Farmers' Depot is misleadingly industrial for such a remote location.
Lens of Sutton

The afternoon train for Haughley, with a posse of enthusiasts aboard, pauses at Kenton behind No. 65447 during the final month of operation. Mixed trains usually travelled 'wrong line'; this passenger-only train was following correct railway practice.
H.N. James

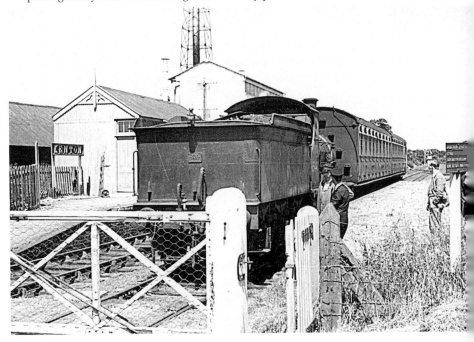

its lasting form it had the air of a bay platform pointing the wrong way. Parallel to it was a shorter siding which between 1912 and 1919 served the engine shed, re-sited plank by plank from its original location beyond the junction for Debenham and finally abandoned when it was decided to stable all the line's locomotives at Laxfield; the shed was eventually cannibalised in 1927. Locomotives had to run into the bay, then reverse into one of two headshunts serving cattle pens and a staithe, before they could set back into the shed. The bay siding joined the up line just before the end of the passing loop, where it threw off a lengthy headshunt roughly level with the point where a further siding from behind the station building converged with the down line after throwing off yet another spur. At the eastern extremity of the yard on the up side stood a sturdy brick-built water tower topped by a tank to which the supply was pumped by a petrol engine, and across the running line the home signal for trains approaching from Laxfield.

Once it was clear the Mid-Suffolk was destined to remain an elongated branch, Kenton, possessing the line's only recognised passing loop, became the token exchange point between its two sections: Haughley to Kenton and Kenton to Laxfield. (It was also possible for trains to pass each other at Gipping and Mendlesham, but neither loop was used for that purpose.) Each section was governed by the novel single divided staff; each staff had two halves, padlocked together except when two trains went through a section in the same direction, as happened thrice weekly in later days. Dr Allen recalled that when an officers' special ran in April 1952 (a 'J15' 0-6-0 with the Ipswich six-wheeled inspection saloon), nobody could enjoy the lunch provided as they could not understand the method of working with split staff and ticket and expected to meet a train coming the other way at any moment.

Kenton's status as the token exchange point also imposed a ritual of its own. To the very end, according to Dr Allen, the two goods guards on the line kept their own individual vans, and when the goods from Laxfield crossed the mixed at Kenton, complicated shunting manoeuvres ensured that when the guards exchanged trains, they also exchanged vans. The upshot was that when the time came for the trains to resume their journey, each left Kenton 'wrong line'.

Kenton to Halesworth

As the excitement of the short-lived junction receded, the line headed north-westwards between more moated farms for two miles before arriving at Worlingworth.

Worlingworth (12 miles)

Sited between the straggling village of Worlingworth to the east and the smaller settlement of Southolt, this station did not attract much traffic despite being closer to human habitation than some others. It was approached from Kenton, six minutes away by most trains, over a level crossing which by the end

Worlingworth station, a typical medium-sized station of the system, seen from the west. In later years, with 'hours' between the trains, life must have been very quiet. *Lens of Sutton*

A close up of the Worlingworth station building. It was surprising but nearly all the MSLR's building structures remained in good condition to the end. *Lens of Sutton*

Worlingworth station at a fractionally busier time. Seen here from the carriage window, looking towards Haughley. *R.M. Casserley*

Horham station looking east, at a rare time when there was pressure of traffic on its siding. For a later view see page 136. *Lens of Sutton*

Horham station, but this time looking towards Haughley. *Lens of Sutton*

Back-to-school for the final year of the 'Middy's' existence? Boyish faces grin and mothers leave the platform as the Haughley train pulls out of Horham, 1st September, 1951. *H.C. Casserley*

was in sorry shape with one of its gates lying on the ground and a rope stretched across the gap with a red flag. Train crews 'opened' it with as much ceremony as the original gate. Worlingworth station had a platform on the down side with a single-bay building with canopy, with a shed on one end and a flat-roofed toilet at the other. Opposite the platform was a siding which in the autumn handled heavy sugar beet traffic, with a short spur facing east.

The line now turned north for the only time, embarking on a 1 in 44 gradient known as Athelington Bank after the closest hamlet. Freight trains working this portion of the line, by contrast with Haughley Bank, were not subject to any restriction - presumably because loads this far down the line were lighter and there was no risk of a runaway endangering main line traffic. As the gradient eased, the line continued through open country close to Athelington itself to reach Horham.

Horham (14 miles)

Serving a smallish village just under half a mile to the north, this was another lightly-used station, though as with Aspall and Kenton there was more goods traffic than could immediately be explained. Five minutes by train from Worlingworth, Horham boasted an identical station building, and one which remained *in situ* until the late 1980s before joining that from Laxfield at Mangapps Farm in Essex. The station platform was on the up side, and the siding opposite abutted quite a substantial goods shed. Like Mendlesham, this station's facilities were strained by extra wartime traffic for a nearby air base - initially asphalt for runway construction and later bombs - with wagons being held occasionally at Gipping until siding space was free. Edna Brown, who worked as a land girl at Laxfield, recalled that US airmen who used the station 'thought it was like a little toy train'.

Leaving Horham over a level crossing, the line swung round to the north-east for the shortest journey between two Mid-Suffolk stations, of fractionally over a mile for which four minutes were allowed. A short embankment was followed by a bridge over a small tributary of the Waveney before the line plunged into one of its very few sections of cutting and, turning more toward the east, entered Stradbroke.

Stradbroke (15 miles)

Prior to the depopulation of the 1870s, Stradbroke might have been slightly larger than Mendlesham, but by the time the Mid-Suffolk assumed its final shape it was the second largest village along its route with a population a little over 900. Solid, with a stately church befitting the small market town it was for so long, Stradbroke lay to the north of its station, its centre being just over half a mile away.

Stradbroke station was the busiest on the line after Haughley and Laxfield, handling substantially more traffic than Mendlesham and keeping more of it when the effects of road competition began to be felt. In common with

Stradbroke station captured on film in very early days just as a train from Haughley and Kenton enters, hauled by locomotive No. 2.

Lens of Sutton

Seen from the west, this view of Stradbroke station shows clearly the space left for installation of a loop had the line's potential been realised. The station building must have been very cramped for the line's clerical staff.

Lens of Sutton

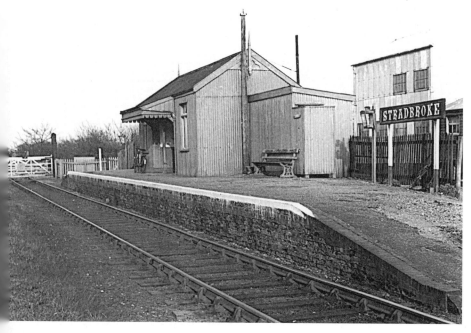

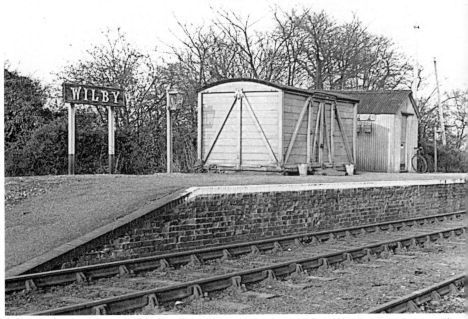

Wilby station, tiniest on the line and very much an afterthought. The station building in the background is now at Brockford.
Lens of Sutton

Rare signs of life at Wilby, which must have been a lonely place to work.
H.C. Casserley

Mendlesham, Stradbroke was vulnerable to bus competition with the railway, each village from an early stage having a daily Eastern Counties service to Ipswich. The bus passed the station on its way out of the village on the road for Framlingham.

The platform, on the up side, accommodated the standard larger Mid-Suffolk station building, of two bays with a canopy and toilets. In latter days the clerical centre of the line, Stradbroke station also had a staff of two for its own purposes. Behind the station building lay two long sidings which handled comparatively heavy traffic, some of it for the agricultural depot beside them. The staithe, cattle pen and spur were also on the up side, at the Kenton end of the station. Room was left at Stradbroke for a passing loop on the down side, should one eventually be needed as the system grew.

Trains leaving Stradbroke immediately crossed the Framlingham road, then headed almost due east through fairly wooded country to the south of the village before crossing open fields to complete a four-minute journey to Wilby.

Wilby (16½ miles)

This station bode fair to be the smallest on the line, not to mention the least used. The small settlement of Wilby lay almost a mile away to the south, and was arguably closer to Stradbroke station in any case. Wilby station was, however, fairly convenient for a small grouping of cottages known as Russell's Green.

Neither opened for freight traffic when goods trains began running in September 1904 nor ready for passengers when they were first carried four years later, Wilby station was an afterthought; hurriedly erected, it opened to traffic in July 1909. This impression is reinforced by its omission from some local maps, by its status as the only Mid-Suffolk station without a cattle pen or loading dock, and by the choice of station buildings: a standard MSLR shed - now at Brockford - which might be original or could have been brought from another station which could spare it, and an old GER van body parked next to it on the platform, on the down side of the running line. Across that line was a single siding with headshunt, which saw little use.

Passengers on the 'Middy' were now nearing the end of their journey. Leaving Wilby station over a level crossing, trains set out on an easy stretch for which they were allowed seven minutes, running just south of east through flat and open country almost parallel with the B1117 Stradbroke-Laxfield road to the north, curving to meet it at Laxfield.

Laxfield (19 miles)

The station that for almost all its life served as the official terminus of the line had, as we have seen, achieved that status by sheer chance, being the last of any size to which track had been laid when construction began to slow. Attractively sited between an orchard and an open field, it lay just outside the village of

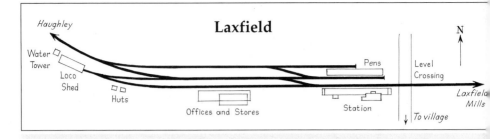

Haughley
Laxfield
N

Water Tower
Loco Shed
Huts
Offices and Stores
Pens
Level Crossing
Station
Laxfield Mills
To village

Laxfield station from beside the line's old headquarters building as No. 65447 awaits the 'right away' with the 1.45 pm to Haughley, 16th April, 1952. *R.M. Casserley*

Surely some mistake. . . the open doors of first class compartments suggest a lucrative traffic on this impending departure from Laxfield behind No. 65459 on 24th September, 1949.
John H. Meredith

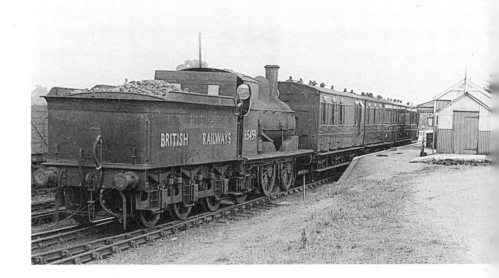

Laxfield at its western extremity, convenient for some but a considerable walk for those of the population of seven to eight hundred who lived at the other end. (Had the line been completed there could well have been a halt at Banyard's Green, the best part of a mile away on the eastern fringe of the village.) Being the terminal point of a railway not only gave Laxfield an added status despite the obscurity of the line (it meant, for instance, that it appeared on British Railways' national route maps while many far larger towns did not); it also gave it a function as a railhead which ensured that the facilities offered were far more heavily used than they would have been at a mere wayside station. This extra traffic and the more complex locomotive and stock movements required at a terminus also taxed a track layout which, as at Kenton, appeared more suited to services to and from Halesworth than on the line as actually operated.

Nevertheless, a wayside stop was exactly what Laxfield seemed. Shortly before the line's closure, H.C. Casserley described the station as 'for all the world like a life-size edition of one of those tinplate model stations provided in one piece for the demonstration by its youthful owner of his table-top model railway', the comparison being all the more appropriate because the station's former office building was actually coated in brick-patterned zinc sheet. Richard Hardy, who as a member of LNER management had probed the mysteries of the engine shed and adjoining buildings, was far less charitable. He wrote that Laxfield depot was the 'most primitive in East Anglia', adding pointedly: 'That was saying something'.

Laxfield became the headquarters of the Mid-Suffolk operation at a time when it was still the expectation, rather than the hope, that the line would be completed, at least to Halesworth. When it became the terminus through chance, it had to house both the administrative and mechanical operations of the company. Quite how the diminutive range of station buildings could have accommodated both the staff employed and the work done is hard to imagine; the eventual move by the LNER of the accounting side to Stradbroke may well have been a humanitarian gesture to all concerned.

Far more traffic was handled at Laxfield than at any other station on the line, especially on the freight side. The regular flow of farm produce and cattle was supplemented between October and December each year by a large amount of sugar beet for the refineries at Ipswich (mainly) and Bury; even in the line's final year of operation (the autumn, 1951 season) 352 wagons of sugar beet were dispatched even though rumours of closure had led some farmers to switch already to road transport. There was also a heavy fruit traffic up to the end. The limited siding accommodation - confirmation that Laxfield was planned as a through station - was thus heavily used.

Throughout the line's active life locomotives approached Laxfield chimney first; the only recorded exceptions are the handful of workings that ran after the official closure. From the footplate the first sign of civilisation was the home signal some little way out protecting the station approaches; toward the end of the line's life the MSLR lower-quadrant signal was replaced by an upper-quadrant of standard LNER design. A couple of hundred yards beyond on the right, just where the run-round loop diverged to the left, was the diminutive engine shed. Designed to accommodate (just) two tank engines and in latter

The passenger end of Laxfield station in the line's final years. Someone has felt the need to chalk the station name over the door of the hut, just in case anyone has missed the nameboard only inches away!   *Real Photographs*

Laxfield station as approached from the village with No. 65447 drawing to a halt in September 1951. The crossing gates had to be closed until the engine had run-round its train.

H.C. Casserley

years housing a 'J15' 0-6-0 with a little to spare, it was of flimsy construction; gaps appeared in the side walls as early as 1912, and in 1951 a storm removed half the roof, which in view of impending closure no-one felt it necessary to replace. A cluster of huts of extreme smallness stood just beyond the shed.

In Mid-Suffolk days, Laxfield depot handled almost all the maintenance and repairs to the company's locomotives, only the heaviest of jobs requiring them to be sent away from the line to Ipswich or, increasingly, to the GER's Stratford works, and to the very end minor repairs were done on the spot, a fitter being summoned from Ipswich when necessary. After the Grouping, engines were sent to Stratford for overhauls and, operationally, Laxfield became a sub-shed of Ipswich (32B). Three locomotives were based there in Mid-Suffolk days (one in turn out-shedded until 1919 at Kenton) and at first under the LNER, but two sufficed during and after World War II. Indeed in the line's closing years No. 65388 spent four days a week in the shed, only being steamed on the other three days for a round-trip goods to Haughley. Only in the sugar beet season was the shed vacated every weekday.

Needless to say, the men of Laxfield shed had not only their own way of doing things, but great pride in their craft. This was especially true after World War II when tender engines arrived on the branch, as there was no turntable the engine had to run tender-first in one direction. Such a service on a long, steep branch with mixed trains and shunting at intermediate stations presented considerable difficulties. But the Laxfield crews managed to run an accelerated service in the line's closing years despite such complications - a tribute both to them and to the ubiquitous 'J15'. The trains ran even faster on Saturday afternoons when Ipswich crews manning the final down working needed to dash from Laxfield to catch a train home from Halesworth or Darsham. One just wonders what driver George Rowse made of it all when he traded in his Garratt banking coal trains up to Woodhead for the bucolic life.

Hard by the engine shed, at the end away from the station, was the water tank belatedly installed there on a timber frame after the contractor was found to have forgotten to make any provision. (Until it was ready, and on occasions throughout the life of the line owing to the vagaries of the supply to it, locomotives had instead to fill up at the pond on the continuation to Laxfield Mills.) The tank from Laxfield shed was destined for further service after the line closed: first at Ipswich, then at Norwich and finally, thanks to the initiative of Mr D.W. Harvey, then shed master at Norwich, on the renascent Festiniog Railway in North Wales. It was transported from Norwich to Tan-y-Bwlch, where until 1969 it made a unique contribution to the preservation movement, supplying water for the station's lavatories.

Laxfield, toward the end, also boasted a water-carrier which was parked in the sidings on the down side. The tender from the former Midland & Great Northern 4-4-0 No. 25 was delivered to the line on 1st January, 1948, the day the railways were nationalised, defiantly bearing newly-painted LNER lettering, and towed away in the final scheduled freight train on 25th July, 1952, going on like the water tank to serve at Ipswich and Norwich. It was finally broken up in 1970, missing preservation by just 24 hours; the M&GN yellow paint was found to be still well preserved under several layers of black.

Nearing the station itself on the up side, incoming trains joined the more southerly of the two lines forking from the shed, then ran alongside a platform bearing a standard 'large' MSLR station building, minus canopy and with a porch onto the platform area, and with a smaller extension in the same style. This was the headquarters of the line in Mid-Suffolk days, from which Mr Gillingwater organised its opening first to goods traffic and then to passenger trains against such formidable odds. When the clerical work of the line was moved to Stradbroke, the superintendent's office became the enginemen's mess, a facility the drivers and firemen must have welcomed given a working day which on Ipswich market days could involve arriving to get up steam at 3 am and damping down after the final service well past 7 pm. These tasks were, of course, performed by separate crews, the first of whom arrived back at Laxfield after two round trips at 10.45 am, clearing the line for the second to make their first run to Haughley at 11.05. Nor was the mess used only for daytime breaks; Mrs Jill Renvoize recalls that her father Ernest Baker, the Ipswich driver in charge of the very last train, used to kip down overnight in what he termed 'the hut' when he had brought in the last train and was booked to be first out in the morning. The same degree of luxury awaited the Ipswich fitter who had occasionally to travel down to work late on repairing one of the line's locomotives. Despite the change of function so long before, the building at the very end still bore the sign 'Superintendent's Office'. The MSLR's original 'headquarters' - covered like the company's Haughley station in brick-patterned zinc sheet - also housed a smith's shop and oil store. Some freight was also handled at its platform.

Some 50 yards beyond stood Laxfield station itself, its platform like others on the line barely able to accommodate two bogie carriages. Closest to the road at the far (eastern) end was a second standard Mid-Suffolk station building, two-bayed with a small canopy and toilets; it outlived the line for three decades before being transported to Bedfield for use as a sports pavilion, then moved again shortly after to the Mangapps Farm railway for eventual use as one of its terminal buildings, along with the MSLR station building from Horham. The Laxfield station nameboard was attached to the side of a shed which took up much of the rest of the platform. These buildings served as booking office, parcels office and waiting room.

On the down side, the loop line threw off a lengthy coal siding parallel to it before rejoining the running line just before the station platform, itself ending in a spur. Between the siding and the spur, close to the road, was a platform on which were a cattle pen and coal staithe.

Although Laxfield boasted run-round facilities, it was never the stated intention of the Mid-Suffolk to make it a passing place for passenger trains had the line been completed, a distinction it shared with Mendlesham. Only one of the platforms constructed was designed to handle passenger trains, whose engines could not run round their coaches without moving them out of the station; the only way two passenger trains could have been handled simultaneously would have been in a 'Cambridge' situation, each on the same running line but with one using the official station platform, and the other the second, freight platform by the superintendent's office. Trains arriving at

Laxfield actually came to rest on or over the level crossing immediately beyond the platform, obstructing the Stradbroke road. With passengers disembarked, they would be backed down the running line to a point level with the former office building. The engine, which might also have to shunt trucks for a mixed train, then set forward, ran back on the loop line to rejoin the running line by the water tank, where it could fill up if the supply were functioning, and then set forward again to rejoin its coaches. It would push these into the station prior to departing for Haughley bunker-first.

Having traversed the level crossing, the line continued in a north-easterly direction on high ground just to the north of Laxfield village. Four hundred yards on was the makeshift water tower erected conveniently close to a pond until a more substantial one could be installed by the engine shed, and which remained in occasional use until the end, locomotives often propelling their carriages down the freight-only branch after running-round. A petrol engine of great antiquity and irregular habits pumped water from the pond into an overhead tank, but in the summer the pond could dry up and a nearby stream, over which the line passed on a small bridge, had to be dammed. Trains must have run here prior to the formal opening of the Cratfield extension, otherwise pond water would have had to be carried to Laxfield station in buckets.

It was an even shorter distance beyond the 'water system', as it was impressively called, to Laxfield Mills.

Laxfield Mills (19½ miles)

As has already been mentioned, this freight siding owed its existence to the negotiation by Mr Goram, owner of the mill, of the right to have goods traffic handled there 'in perpetuity' in return for giving up lands for the onward construction of the line. A single siding was provided, trailing from the 'main' line, and no railway buildings. The Mills were fractionally more convenient for the centre of Laxfield than was the actual station, but while the odd joy-rider may have been carried there, the limited access to the site over Mr Goram's drive - not to mention the spectacular infrequency of trains - did not encourage casual passengers to try their luck. Traffic handled at the Mills, in later years a potato store, was always light, but because of the terms of the agreement it continued to the very end, the depot forming the end of the line as worked from 1912 until 1952; on the final few hundred yards the MSLR flat-bottomed rail was never replaced by bullhead and survived to the very end.

The headshunt at Laxfield Mills continued for a couple of hundred yards further over a small farm track - the final 'occupation' crossing and the least hazardous on the line - before 'petering out uneventfully into a maze of bushes', as an explorer at the time of closure put it. In fact a pile of rotting sleepers denoted the very end of the line, the gang who took up the rails of the Cratfield extension lacking the heart or the finances to erect a set of buffers.

From 1905 until around 1916 (actually being in use from 1906 to 1912) the line continued in a north-westerly direction for at least a further mile and a half. Some 600 yards beyond Laxfield Mills came the level crossing near Banyard's

Above: Laxfield Mills in 1949, seen from the Cratfield direction. Note the flat-bottomed track spiked to the sleepers, also the lack of trucks in the siding which was always lightly used. *John H. Meredith*

Right: No. 65388 makes the very last visit to Laxfield Mill in June 1953. *Dr Ian C. Allen*

Below: The very end of the line! *Dr Ian C. Allen*

Green at which point a halt might have served the east of Laxfield (though much of the building near to it came in the line's later years). Continuing just south of the present-day power lines, the 'Middy' at its fullest extent crossed the drive of Cratfield Red House farm through two holes in the hedge, and over the Cratfield-Heveningham road by a more substantial crossing to reach Cratfield.

Cratfield (21 miles)

Intended as a station for passengers as well as freight, this was as far as the working railway ever got, receiving sporadic goods trains for almost six years as hopes of reaching Halesworth tailed away. It is probably no coincidence that it marked almost the exact point where the line had to abandon its snake-like path over gentle slopes for more sharply undulating terrain through which small rivers cut their way to the coast. From this point onwards, substantial earthworks were far more frequently required, and Jackson's appear to have been singularly loath to tackle them.

While occasional 'unofficial' passengers may have travelled from Cratfield at their own risk, the station would have been lightly used even had the line been completed. The village, half a mile away to the north, is small and the promoters' hopes must have rested largely on agricultural traffic - especially fruit for markets in London and Yorkshire which was handled in some quantity during the station's brief life. Yet the most spectacular consignment handled was of a very different magnitude: a special train in late 1908 or early 1909 bringing the contents of an entire farm from Wisbech on behalf of a farmer who was moving into the area.

The station layout at Cratfield comprised a running line with a siding, of which no details survive. A platform was constructed and on it, a standard MSLR shed. The story goes that a local farmer was told to collect a hen-house that had been delivered for him and took away the station building in error; it must have been returned, for after passing through various hands following closure the Mid-Suffolk Light Railway Society now has it in safe keeping. One day, maybe, it will adorn a reconstructed platform at Aspall. Certainly most traces of the railway at Cratfield vanished in short order once services had been withdrawn and the line lifted, though in 1987 Mr M.J. Richards of Woodbridge found 'evidence of a small embankment now covered in bushes near the site of the old Cratfield station, an obvious old railway working'.

By all accounts the Mid-Suffolk metals finally came to an end close to the 21¼ mile point, some 350 yards beyond Cratfield station on high ground amid open fields. The course of the line continued to be fenced off for about a mile further, close to the point where the varying routes into Halesworth diverged.

The course the line was following at this point was a little to the south of the route originally planned; however its direction was not in doubt. Just over half a mile beyond Cratfield it was to swing due east and head across open country for the next station at Huntingfield.

Possibly the only surviving photograph of the Mid-Suffolk at its eastern extremity of Cratfield. Reputedly taken there in 1906 and now proudly displayed in the village inn, 'The Poacher', it shows *Lady Stevenson* arriving or departing with a group of workmen, watched by smarter dressed locals.   *MSLR Co.*

Huntingfield (22½ miles)

Several hundred yards north of this small, straggling village up a sleepy, climbing lane, the siting of this projected station did not please local opinion, and at a very early stage villagers led by their rector petitioned the Light Railway Commissioners to have it brought nearer.

The promoters of the line provided for a loop at Huntingfield, which would apparently have been the only one on the 'main' line apart from that at Kenton designated for passenger trains to pass. The implication of this is that in service, trains between Kenton and Halesworth would have crossed here rather than at Laxfield, where the loop would have been used for shunting only as at Gipping and Mendlesham, with Huntingfield station being protected in each direction by home signals of the MSLR lower-quadrant variety. The final stretch from Huntingfield to Halesworth (where run-round facilities were of course planned) would have been a further section in its own right.

It was the attempted construction of this final section that caused the Mid-Suffolk company so much trouble and contributed mightily to its failure. Three different approaches to a junction with the Great Eastern at Halesworth were proposed, namely the original (1900)* route south of the town to a terminus on the west side of the East Suffolk line at the south of the GER station; the 1903 and 1909 route skirting the north of Halesworth to a terminus on the west side of the East Suffolk line at the south of the GER station; and the 1907 route south of the town, crossing the Great Eastern to join the Southwold Railway's route into Halesworth, ending at a separate station east of both the other lines. It is probably least confusing to outline them in turn, starting from Huntingfield as they all diverged not far beyond that station.

The Original (1900) Route

The approach to Halesworth outlined in the company's Prospectus was the longest of the three proposed, though on paper the most straightforward. The line, from Huntingfield station, was to run due east through a covert just to the south of the small village of Cookley, where a bridge over a lane was envisaged, hugging the 100 ft contour and requiring a considerable embankment as it. approached Walpole.

Walpole (24 miles)

This final intermediate station was to be sited just to the north of this small village, at the confluence of the River Blyth and a tributary, arms of which the line had already crossed at Laxfield and Cratfield. The works at Walpole were to be considerable, involving two bridges.

Beyond Walpole the route was to describe a gentle curve to the north-east as it descended to approach the Great Eastern main line from Ipswich for the final stretch into Halesworth. Just at the convergence, by Mells brickyard, was to be

* The plans for each were actually lodged the year before that stated.

-B-

— G.E.R. HALESWORTH

— PROPOSED ACCOMODATION FOR MID-SUFFOLK LIGHT RAILWAY —

AT YARMOUTH END OF STATION

RESERVOIR

1 in 70

1 in 88

Scale 66 Feet = 1 Inch

NOTE— G.E.R COMPANY'S BOUNDARY
IS EDGED GREEN.

G.E.R MAIN LINE

FOOTPATH

LEVEL CROSSING

BUNGAY

ROAD

Signal Box

Plan of MSLR station at Halesworth proposed under the 1903 deviation scheme.

a level crossing, plans for which caused local councillors concern when the route was first published. The proposal was for the Mid-Suffolk, just yards to the west of a crossing on the existing line, to have a separate crossing with its own gates. However Blything council took the view that horse-drawn vehicles could be trapped between the two crossings and that the beasts might panic before either line was clear. Thus it was decided that one set of gates would suffice for both crossings, despite the distance between them.

From Mells brickyard the Mid-Suffolk was to run beside the Great Eastern metals, by now on an embankment over water meadows where the Blyth acquired one of its main tributaries, for the run of three-quarters of a mile into Halesworth. It was the burden on the Mid-Suffolk company of duplicating the GER's earthworks on this marshy stretch that was cited as the main reason for abandoning this approach to the town. As the terminus was finally reached, the Mid-Suffolk line would veer slightly to the west to a separate station at Halesworth.

Halesworth (27¾ miles)

This was to be sited beside maltings at the south end of the existing main line station, with a trailing connection to the GER. Sidings already on the site would have had to be remodelled both to make way for the new line and to cater for exchange traffic.

It should be noted here that Halesworth station, quite apart from its picturesque function as a terminus of the narrow gauge Southwold line, was remarkable in itself. The main road running northward out of the town (the A144 to Bungay) ran not only close to the station buildings at the north end, but bisected each of the two platforms. The Great Eastern's solution to enable trains of more than five or six coaches to be served was to have a level crossing constructed bearing platform sections, the entire device on both up and down platforms swinging round to enable road traffic to cross the line, then returning when a train was due to connect with platform extensions stretching north. In 1922 a more sophisticated platform crossing of all-metal construction was installed; it is still *in situ* but no longer swings open, as the road now crosses the East Suffolk line on a bridge to the north of the station. Paradoxically the platform extension is no longer needed either, as Halesworth is now served solely by the shortest of 'paytrains', having lost its last through locomotive-hauled service to Liverpool Street in 1984.

The Northern Route (1903 and 1909)

The second line promoted to reach Halesworth broke from the originally planned route three-quarters of a mile east of Huntingfield station, swinging over a river and road crossing on an embankment to a station varyingly named Cookley and Walpole.

Cookley or Walpole (23½ miles)

The stop was extremely convenient for the former community but some way from the latter, which being larger could have provided more traffic. Its naming could have been a sop to the villagers of Walpole for the loss of the far closer station they had originally been promised.

From here the line, having fallen already from 214 ft at the top of Haughley Bank to the 100 ft contour, was to begin a further descent as it ran just north of east, north of the Blyth toward the 26 mile mark. By this point it would have been heading due north, prior to commencing a tight curve describing a semi-circle round the town of Halesworth to reach its terminus. The earthworks on this final stretch were daunting, as the company and its contractors found when work got under way, with at least one bridge and maybe as many as three being required. Most of the surviving traces of this activity, and notably the trackbed of the trailing connection with the Great Eastern to which that company had grudgingly agreed, were eliminated when the area to the north-west of the main line station was redeveloped in the 1970s; an embankment carrying the A144 now runs across the course of both lines, and building work just north of it removed further traces.

Halesworth (26¾ miles)

The MSLR's proposed northern terminus at Halesworth would have been even more conveniently sited for through passengers than that first proposed, lying just across the road from the GER building. Run-round facilities and an exchange siding were once again planned, with a connection to the main line of some complexity. The Great Eastern's fears that trucks awaiting transfer might run away onto its route to the north and cause a serious accident led the MSLR to propose a zig-zag on whose central portion wagons could safely be parked.

The Southwold Route (1907)

By far the most confusing of the three courses proposed, this route bears all the hallmarks of desperation by a company seeing its goal within sight but out of reach. As far as can be established, it was also the only one with no intermediate station between Huntingfield and Halesworth.

Breaking with the original route at the same point as the 1905 alternative, it struck out slightly north of east on a course roughly bisecting the angle between those previously promoted. Crossing the river and its parallel road a little way east of Cookley, it ran just north of Walpole but out of reach across the valley, continuing on the northern side of the Blyth until the town of Halesworth hove in sight. The route now proposed skirted the town almost a mile to the south, appearing set to miss it altogether as it crossed to the south bank of the river. At the 25¾ mile mark a 'stopping place' was prescribed, presumably as an assurance to the Southwold company that trains which had made the prolonged descent from Huntingfield would not be speeding out of control as they approached its tracks, and also because of the sharpness of the bend ahead.

Just north of the brickworks and a good half-mile south of Halesworth station, the Mid-Suffolk was to pass under the Great Eastern at right angles, before almost immediately swinging round 90 degrees to run due north. Quite what was to happen beyond this point was never entirely clear; all the Southwold Directors knew was that they did not like it, and the Light Railway Commissioners appear to have shared their and the Great Eastern's misgivings. At the 26¼ mile point, the briefest of branches was to be thrown off toward Southwold, with the 'main' Mid-Suffolk line continuing to make a triangular junction with that railway's route as it prepared to enter Halesworth. Even if the Mid-Suffolk and Southwold tracks could be kept separate as they neared their end, the only possible inference behind the short spur proposed to run eastward was a future change of the Southwold line from 3 ft to standard gauge so that Mid-Suffolk trains could reach the coast without reversing. The Great Eastern's fears about that, and a possible tie-up between the Mid-Suffolk and the predatory Midland Railway, have already been rehearsed.

As far as can be ascertained, the Mid-Suffolk's final stretch would have run beside the Southwold's single track over Holton Road and into the Halesworth station area before cutting across to a separate station on the eastern side of the other two companies.

Halesworth (MSLR) (27 miles)

The siting of the MSLR station under this arrangement would have required not only a mixed gauge crossover on the approach to the terminus but also careful siting of both the connection to the GER main line and the exchange sidings. One can only assume they would have been some little way south of Halesworth station, at which point the Mid-Suffolk track would have run between those of the other two companies. The only other logical thought is that once again it was assumed that the Southwold Railway could somehow be induced to change its gauge as part of a grander and unstated scheme.

With the benefit of hindsight, the Mid-Suffolk company accepted that this scheme was a non-runner and went back to the admittedly costly proposals of 1903 for the northern route. But the time lost had been fatal, the powers for construction lapsed and Halesworth was never reached. The Southwold line closed in 1929 and the former junction now enjoys a purely local service as far as Lowestoft only; the direct Yarmouth route was closed in the late 1950s, the few remaining through trains from London being diverted via Norwich, and the Lowestoft-Yarmouth branch which lingered on for a further decade is now at its northern end the course of a road. The approach to Halesworth on the main line from Yarmouth, where the Great Eastern feared exchange shunting and even runaways on the stiff gradient would hazard its own busy service, has now been reduced to single track.

Halesworth (GER) station looking south, with the platform/level crossing gate half open. The MSLR station planned under the 1903 and 1909 (northern route) proposals would have been immediately to the right and that proposed originally, to the right beyond the footbridge. The Southwold Railway platform is out of sight to the left of the signal box; the MSLR station proposed in the 1907 route would have been beyond that. *Lens of Sutton*

The Aspall Road bridge just north of Debenham with the substantial embankment on either side, the only traces surviving of the short-lived Debenham branch. *Author*

Southward from Kenton

The two mile section of track from Kenton to just north of Debenham may only have handled an informal freight traffic for three short years, but in that time it boasted two separate routes out of the junction. At the outset and probably until just before the branch's closure in 1906, trains left Kenton on the same single track as the 'main' service to and from Haughley. Just beyond the station level crossing was a passing loop of particular use to the contractor, for *Lady Stevenson* could run round its construction train before heading down the branch with men or supplies. The junction for Debenham at first was 200 yards out of Kenton, the branch leaving the engine shed to the right and served by a spur from the 'main' line.

Once the line from Haughley was open for goods traffic, trains for Debenham gained an exit of their own from Kenton - though not from the south face of the station's island platform as would have been logical and indeed was provided for in the pre-1905 layout disapproved of by the Board of Trade. They set off from the north face on the same up line as trains bound for Haughley, but where the station loop ended just beyond the double track level crossing they gained a track of their own, running alongside the 'main line' for 200 yards until it swung away to westward by the engine shed on the original contractor's alignment. When the branch was lifted during World War I, the first 170 yards to just before the point where it diverged was kept as a siding, giving the illusion of double track.

Continuing south-westward for a further mile, the branch then ran into hilly country which continued almost uninterrupted to Westerfield, and which - like the line beyond Cratfield - served as a deterrent to the contractor. The next three-quarters of a mile involved the heaviest earthworks actually constructed anywhere on the Mid-Suffolk system, almost all of which are still in place 80 years after the lifting of the track.

As it began a gentle curve by the end of which it was running due south, the line ran onto a sizeable embankment some 400 yards in length, halfway along which was a bridge over the B1077 Aspall Road. Despite the distance of the bridge from Debenham - the best part of a mile - Peter Paye has discovered that the MSLR company purchased a 500 ft by 300 ft plot of land just to the south of it as the possible site of a station and goods yard to serve the village. To site the station there would have been a council of desperation, and there is no sign that any work was undertaken.

Not far beyond the road, the embankment gave way to a shallow cutting as it sliced through the top of a hill on the north-west fringe of Debenham. As the ground fell away, a lane rose sharply to cross the line of route, just past the 2 mile mark from Kenton. Contemporary maps show the line continuing to just beyond this point. Gates to the premises on the north side of the lane suggest a railway origin, and freight could have been handled in a yard abutting a stretch of trackbed where saplings are now reared in a small nursery. To the south of the lane a further substantial embankment was constructed, stopping just short of a brook and a lane named 'The Butts', which was to have been bridged. Beyond this was a second site, 400 ft by 120 ft, bought by the company to be the station for Debenham.

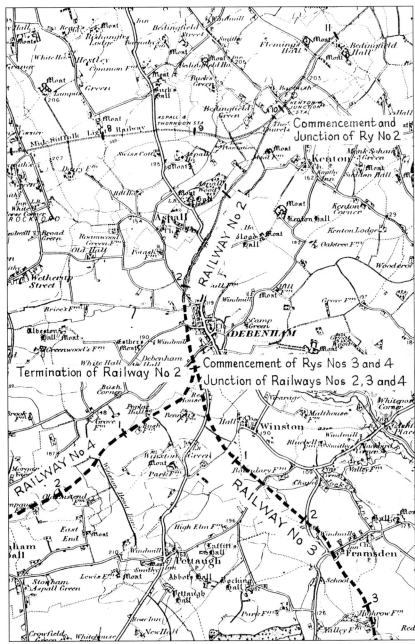

The original 1899 plan for lines in the Debenham area, showing the divergence of the swiftly abandoned Needham Market route. The earthworks for the Debenham branch continued almost to the station site. *Reproduced from the 1", 1906 Ordnance Survey Map*

Debenham (2½ miles)

Debenham, a small hilly town full of character, would have been the largest settlement on the Mid-Suffolk system (Halesworth apart), its population never having fallen below 1,000 even at the worst of the agricultural depression. The railway company was determined to gain the traffic from it, siting the more convenient of the two projected stations just 200 yards from its centre and regarding abandonment of the line from Kenton as reversible as late as 1909. But although the contractor actually had his office there, the prospect of the heavy engineering works required to push through and past Debenham and on to the south was too much for the firm. Little is known of what was planned for the station there, but while it would have been logical for there to have been a loop, it might well have been for shunting only as at Mendlesham, rather than signalled for service trains to cross as Kenton was so close at hand.

Beyond the station and now running due south, the line was to pass under the B1115 Stowmarket road. Almost immediately beyond was the point where the early-discarded Needham Market branch would have split away. That line would have been the least costly and difficult to construct of all those originally planned, having apparently involved no earthworks or bridges at all. It would have struck out south-westward to pass, three miles on, just to the north of the village of Stonham Aspal where one imagines there would have been a station (plans for this branch were not developed to the point where stopping places were specified). At the four-mile point it was to cross the A140 Ipswich-Norwich road on the level between the villages of Little Stonham and Earl Stonham, close to where there would almost certainly have been a further station. Rather less likely would have been a station at the 6-mile point, where the lane from Creeting St Mary, a little to the south, would have crossed the line. A freight-only siding, as at Gipping, would, however, have been a possibility. Six and a half miles from the junction with the Westerfield route and 9¼ from Kenton, the branch was to swing southward for its final stretch into Needham Market beside the River Gipping.

Needham Market (10½ miles from Kenton)

The line's terminal point would have been on the site of sidings to the east of the GER station, with a trailing connection between the two lines. Needham Market was the only junction planned with the Great Eastern which was not also served by other lines: Haughley and Westerfield marked the convergence of two Great Eastern routes while Halesworth also played host to the Southwold Railway. Needham Market enjoyed a passenger service of much the same frequency as Haughley, but in the view of the line's promoters had a special advantage as grain traffic from points on the MSLR for the maltings by Needham Market station could be carried without the need for transfer to the Great Eastern. Yet when forced by the Commissioners to choose between this terminal and Haughley, they had little hesitation in discarding Needham Market.

CROSS SECTION Nº 8

1 in 31·7

RAIL LEVEL

Greatest inclination of Present Road 1 in 31·4

CROSS SECTION Nº 1

1 in 111

RAIL LEVEL

Greatest inclination of Present Road 1 in 111

— RAILWAY Nº 3 – 5 M. 2 F. 4·5 Chs. TO 8 M. OF. 5 Chs. —

O T L E Y   P A R I S H

S W I L L A N D   P A R I S H

W I T N E S H A M

C O U N T Y   O F   S U F F O L K

Deviation

Deviation

Gravel Lane 3 M 1 F 9·5 Chs Level Crossing

Public Road Level Crossing

Occupation Road Level Crossing

Public Road Level Crossing

Occupation Road Level Crossing

Public Road Level Crossing

Occupation Road Level Crossing

Public Road Level Crossing

Occupation Road Level Crossing

Public Road Level Crossing Nº 9

Occupation Road Level Crossing

1 in 700

1 in 55

1 in 160

1 in 50

1 in 30

1 in 153

1 in 225

1 in 280

1 in 50

1 in 54

1 in 182

1 in 105

Revised plans and gradients profile for the Otley section of the Westerfield branch c. 1903.

Suffolk County Archives

Meanwhile the Westerfield line would have run, and the fencing for it actually did, south-east of south from Debenham, the limit of land actually acquired by the company being passed at 3¾ miles. Its course left the hamlet of Winston - in modern times the home of the Cabinet Minister John Gummer - to the left, reaching its next station at Framsden.

Framsden (5¼ miles)

This smaller station, convenient for the village, would have been on one of the more heavily-engineered sections of the line, with a bridge on one road and a further one under another. Beyond it, the line was to continue due south again, climbing steadily, as the B1077 to Ipswich disappeared to the right. Originally the plan was to pass next well to the east of the small village of Helmingham, but after representations from landowners (against the original proposals, not seeking a more convenient service) it was shifted almost half a mile to the west, with a station fairly close to Helmingham.

Helmingham (7¼ miles)

This again would have been a minor stopping place, though traffic to and from Helmingham Hall, whose drive reached to the centre of the village, might have brought a touch of class to the line.

Shortly beyond Helmingham station, where there was to have been a level crossing over the B1069 for Woodbridge, the branch was to reach the highest point on the system: 218 ft, or just 4 ft higher than the top of Haughley Bank. From here it was to be steadily downhill to Westerfield. A swerve to the south-west and then south again brought the course of the branch to Otley.

Otley (8¾ miles)

This would have been one of the Mid-Suffolk's larger stations, enjoying with Kenton and Huntingfield the privilege of a passing loop for passenger trains. The village it was to serve was one of the largest in the district and a promising source of connecting traffic for Ipswich, but difficulties with landowners forced the line and station away from the built-up area; the average inhabitant of this straggling village would have faced a walk of nearly a mile. The station was to have been squeezed between two level crossings, with access from its southern end.

From here the line was to continue due south, past the hamlet of Swilland, on a steady downward grade including one short stretch at 1 in 50 and two at 1 in 55 to Witnesham.

Witnesham (10½ miles)

Three-quarters of a mile east of the village, the siting of the station aroused protests from local people which were of no avail. Just to the north of the station, a bridge over the lane leading to Witnesham village was planned. Continuing southward for a mile, the line was then to swing south-west to reach Tuddenham siding.

Tuddenham Siding (12¼ miles)

No passenger service was ever planned at this stop, close to the small community of the same name. Indeed the only evidence that any kind of station was envisaged comes in the company's Minutes for early 1902 when the contractor is being instructed to start work. The Board determined that he should start at Westerfield and move towards 'the proposed Tuddenham siding'. One imagines that the traffic handled would have been light, on a par with that to and from Gipping.

From Tuddenham, the route ran south-west in a straight line for three-quarters of a mile before a final curve into Westerfield.

Westerfield (MSLR) (13½ miles)

With the terminal track running east and west, the Mid-Suffolk station would have been to the north of the GER premises and below them, on a site now occupied by a haulage depot. Alone of the four junctions with the 'main line' planned at the outset, it would have had a facing connection with Great Eastern metals. However, as that company was still arguing well into 1903 about these arrangements, little can be regarded as having been settled. Indeed in the case of Westerfield, the delay in getting on with the job was probably as much the responsibility of an unenthusiastic GER as of the errant contractor.

Westerfield GER station was, and remains, the junction of the East Suffolk line and that to Felixstowe. In times gone by it possessed not only its two through platforms but a double bay on the up side for branch traffic, with a picturesque seaside-type wooden station building, originally the terminus for trains of the Felixstowe Railway, acquired by the Great Eastern in 1885 after its flirtation with the Midland. With the connection planned, Mid-Suffolk trains from Kenton, freight and excursion alike, could have traversed the main line onto the Felixstowe branch with just one reversal . . . or indeed run straight through to Ipswich, just 3½ miles further on, as they were to beyond Haughley to Stowmarket in the line's final years. Sidings which were already in place on the up side could have handled exchange traffic.

Today there is no sign (if ever there was) that Westerfield could have been a junction of three routes; all but the running lines have gone though the old Felixstowe Railway building remains, well over a century after the line lost its independence.

Chapter Five

Retrenchment and Grouping

Though the Mid-Suffolk Board would have been loath to admit it, 1912 was the year when the dream of reaching Halesworth faded and the line took on the form it was to retain until closure four decades later. The decisive event was the abandonment that February of the freight-only section between Laxfield Mills and Cratfield, traffic on which had fallen well short of covering costs. The track was kept *in situ* in the hope that the line might yet be completed, but the halting of trains over a mile and a half of the planned Halesworth extension must have made it clearer than ever before that goal was unlikely to be reached.

Meanwhile the main concern of the Mid-Suffolk management was to make the best of what railway they had, and to operate it in the most economical fashion. The system of working was now adopted that was to persist until the very end on days when there was more than one engine in steam: the division of the line at Kenton into two sections each worked by the split staff. In each section the complete staff (or one or other portion of it) had to be carried by each train entering the single line. When a train was setting out and none other was scheduled before the return journey, the complete staff was handed to the driver. If another was to follow before the staff could be returned, the staff was divided and the 'ticket half' given to the first driver. The second train carrying the 'train half' would not be allowed to set out until it could be confirmed by telephone that the first was out of section. On arrival at the end of a section, the driver handed in whichever portion of the staff he had to the official (there were no signalmen) with the responsibility for screwing the portions together and locking them with the key provided; whatever further movements were planned, the staff had first to be reassembled as a precaution against mishap.

The pattern of services now settled down, the only question being on which days and for how much of its run the midday train carried passengers as well as freight. The summer timetable for 1913, for example, showed two passenger trains in each direction on weekdays, plus a further departure from Kenton to Haughley on Tuesdays, Wednesdays and Thursdays with no published balancing working. The Sunday timetable operated during August only, still with two trains in each direction.

Despite the withdrawal from Cratfield, the MSLR management had not yet given up hope of completing the line to Halesworth, and with powers for constructing the remaining portion on the point of expiry asked the Board of Trade about the prospects of extending the time limit. The reply was not encouraging: there was no way an extension would be granted if the line remained in receivership, and on the face of it the chances of selling the undertaking were bleak. Meanwhile the debenture holders had reached the conclusion that there was no chance of their getting their money back with the line as it stood (the more so after the retreat from Cratfield), and applied to the Board of Trade for consent to the sale of the undertaking. What they had in mind was that a new company, whose promoters they professed to be in touch

MID - SUFFOLK LIGHT RAILWAY

SERVICE TIME TABLE - MARCH 10TH. 1919 AND UNTIL FURTHER NOTICE.

U P   T R A I N S

Train numbers		1	2	3	4	5	6	7	8	Sundays 9-
Description		Ctl. Tue. Only	Gds. Mon. and Thu. Only	Mxd. Dly.	Gds. Mon. Only	Gds. Tue. and Thu. Only	Gds. Wed. Fri. Sat. Only	Mxd. Tue. and Thu. Only	Mxd. Dly.	Pass.
		a.m.	a.m.	a.m.	a.m.	a.m.	a.my	p.m.	p.m.	p.m.
LAXFIELD	dep.	4. 0		8.15				12.55	3.25	6.15
Wilby	"	B		8.23	9C35	9C35	9C35	1. 3	3.33	6.23
Stradbroke	"	B		8.28	9.45	9.45	9.45	1. 8	3.40	6.28
Horham	"	B		8.33	A	A	A	1.13	3.47	6.32
Worlingworth	"	B		8.39	A	A	A	1.20	3.54	6.38
KENTON	arr.	4.45		8.45	10.25	10.25	10.25	1.26	4. 2	6.46
KENTON	dep.	4.55	5.45	8.46		10C40	10.55	1.33	4. 3	6.47
Aspall	"	A	A	8.53	A	A	A	1.40	4.15	6.51
Brockford	"	A	A	9. 2	A	A	A	1.47	4.22	6.59
Mendlesham	"	B	A	9. 8		-	A	1.55	4.28	7. 4
Gipping Siding	"	-	-	-	-	-	-	-	-	-
HAUGHLEY	arr.	5.45	6.45	9.23		11C25	11.55	2.10	4.42	7.17
G. E. R. connecting train		wai- ting	7.30	9.34		1.30	1.30	2.29	5. 8	7.26
Engine working		K	K	L	K	K	K	LK	L	L

A - Stops when required.   B - Stops to attach cattle only.
C - Runs when required.   K - Kenton engine.
         L - Laxfield engine.

D O W N   T R A I N S

Train numbers		10	11	12	13	14	15	16	17	18	Sundays 19
G. E. R. connecting train		5.30	5.30		9.51	10. 0	10C 0		1.30	5.33	7.36
Description		Gds. Tue. Only	Gds. Mon. and Thu. Only	Gds. Wed. Fri. Sat. Only	Mxd. Dly.	Gds. Tue. and Thu. Only	Gds. Wed. Fri. Sat. Only	Eng. Tue. and Thu. Only	Gds. Tue. and Thu. Only	Mxd. Dly.	Pass.
		a.m.	a.m.	a.m.	a.m.	p.m.	p.m.	p.m.	p.m.	p.m.	p.m.
HAUGHLEY	dep.	7. 0	7.30		10. 0	12C15	1.10		2.55	5.40	7.40
Gipping Siding	"	-	-		-	-	A		A	-	-
Mendlesham	"	A	A		10.13	-	A		A	5.54	7.54
Brockford	"	A	B		10.19	-	A		A	5.59	7.59
Aspall	"	A	B		10.27	-	A		A	6. 7	8. 7
KENTON	arr.	8. 0	8.15		10.31	12C50	2.10		3.55	6.11	8.11
KENTON	dep.	8.46	8.46	8.46	10.32			1.30		6.12	8.12
Worlingworth	"	B	B	-	10.40			-		6.20	8.20
Horham	"	A	A	A	10.50			-		6.26	8.26
Stradbroke	arr.	9.10	9.10	9.10							
Stradbroke	dep.	9C25	9C25	9C25	10.55			-		6.30	8.30
Wilby	arr.	9C30	9C30	9C30							
Wilby	dep.				11. 0			-		6.35	8.35
LAXFIELD	arr.				11.10			2. 0		6.42	8.42
Engine working		K	K	K	L	K	K	L	K	L	L

A - Stops when required.   B - Stops to attach cattle only.
C - Runs when required.   K - Kenton engine.
         L - Laxfield engine.

The highly complex working timetable devised by Mr Lindsey-Badcock for the Spring of 1919.   *GER Society*

with, would buy out the debenture holders for £45,000 (half as much again as the LNER eventually paid for the entire line and three times what the debenture holders were to receive) and complete the route itself.

The Board of Trade declared itself powerless in a matter where quite clearly the Receiver and the debenture holders were at loggerheads. There was nothing in the Light Railway Act to allow the sale of a line in such circumstances to a private bidder; while sale to a local authority was permissible in some circumstances, the Order setting up the Mid-Suffolk did not make any provision for it. The dissident shareholders next tried their luck with the MSLR Board, which was still pursuing a sporadic and shadowy existence (though there was nothing shadowy about the losses the Directors had suffered: the Earl of Stradbroke nearly £5,000 when a reckoning was finally made and Mr Remnant and Mr Cobbold, by now not an active member, over £3,000 each). It emerged that there was a chance of a Halesworth Light Railway Company being formed to take over the Mid-Suffolk and obtain powers of its own to complete the line, on terms that would satisfy major debenture holders though not necessarily the company's other creditors. Soundings were taken, and as late as September 1914, one month into World War I, there was still an outside chance of the deal coming to fruition.

On the outbreak of war the fortunes of the Mid-Suffolk were as sound as the continuing failure to complete the line or pay off the burden of debt would permit; to the satisfaction of management, traffic had been increasing steadily. With the advent of wartime controls, the Mid-Suffolk company was notified by the War Office that it was one of the 130 railway undertakings out of 176 which had been taken over by the Government for the duration. While the line might not have appeared crucial to the war effort, it did serve an area that might be prone to a German invasion; this explanation would have been more convincing had not the Felixstowe Dock and Railway Company, clearly a prime target, remained outside State control. Government ownership in wartime assisted the Mid-Suffolk management through the provision of subsidies for services deemed essential, among them trains run to convey the Scottish troops drafted into the area to build defensive lines. While the subsidies came in handy, they were not without strings; the Ministry of Transport later found grounds for claiming much of them back.

Wartime did bring one moment of high drama to the line which, regrettably, passed almost unchronicled. On the night of 2nd/3rd September, 1916, thirteen Zeppelins flew over East Anglia to conduct one of the heaviest raids of the war, and one scored an almost direct hit on the line between Gipping and Mendlesham. The same raid inflicted considerable damage on the Great Eastern system, notably at Stratford and Liverpool Street, but the Mid-Suffolk's own solitary bomb, dropped just after three in the morning, not to mention the clearing up afterwards, must have come as a rude shock.

There was little further talk of extension once the war was in progress, the proposed Halesworth Light Railway takeover fizzling out amid graver concerns. The retrenchment already practised went a stage further when the decision was taken to lift some 3½ miles of now disused track, from the end of the headshunt at Kenton to the outskirts of Debenham and from Laxfield Mills to Cratfield. It took until well into 1916 to complete the work as labour could not easily be spared. Most of the metals were sold for scrap to the armaments industry though a few did get a new lease of life on the Glasgow Underground; the sleepers were sold to local farmers or for firewood.

In July 1913 the Mid-Suffolk company had abruptly dispensed with the services of the energetic Mr Gillingwater amid hints of misdemeanour and possible legal action; Mr W. Lindsey-Badcock took over as both general superintendent and Engineer, also replacing Mr Szlumper. The running of the line was now largely in the hands of Major Daniel, well into his eighties, and Mr Lindsey-Badcock, who stayed until his death at the early age of 52 just before the line was taken over by the LNER. One of his last letters from his home in Stowmarket was a request to the new company for the terms of the settlement; the railway returned his postal order for 2s. 3d. because it was not yet completed. Trained as an engineer on Plymouth docks, Mr Lindsey-Badcock joined the Chief Engineer's staff on the Great Western in 1899, moving directly from there to the Mid-Suffolk. As the author of several papers on railway operation, his reputation extended well beyond the line, whose traffic notices and other instructional material bore his clear stamp. On his death Mr Dalgleish, who had been assistant superintendent since 1905, took over as acting superintendent. Early in 1918 Major Daniel finally resigned as Receiver, shortly before his death at the age of 89, and after a year-long interregnum Mr Alexander Parker, assistant manager of the Great Eastern, succeeded him on an acting basis. In 1921 the Earl of Stradbroke finally gave up the thankless post of company Chairman, Mr Remnant being elected in his place despite having moved to Essex and Mr Parker being invited to join the Board. Mr Chevallier was still using the first class saloon from Aspall on Ipswich market days; in 1919 he tried to interest the County Council and various Government departments in completing the line to Halesworth, but to no avail.

The return of peace found the Mid-Suffolk operating as complicated a timetable as it was ever to handle. Mr Lindsey-Badcock had devised a structure of different services over varying parts of the route on particular days to meet traffic needs with, for instance, a goods train from the Haughley direction terminating at Stradbroke each day, with an optional extension to Wilby, before returning. In March 1919 there were as before the war two mixed trains each way with, now, an extra up train all the way from Laxfield every Tuesday and Thursday. There was a Sunday service throughout the year of one train each way, leaving Laxfield at 6.15 pm and being back by 8.45. There was still an engine shedded at Kenton and some trains started from there, but the shed was closed that autumn.

The Sunday train finally disappeared in 1921, and the rest of the timetable was simplified. Mixed trains left Laxfield at 7.35 am (8.10 on Tuesdays), 11.05 (third class only) and 3.25 pm; there were return journeys from Haughley at 9.40 am, 12.55 pm (third class only) and 5.40 pm. Goods workings had also been rationalised: one each way early on Tuesdays, another each way as required and a daily working from Laxfield to Aspall and back. Kenton was the only scheduled stop for freight trains, as much because of the need to tie in with other trains at the only passing place as through the volume of traffic the former junction generated; all other stations were to be called at 'when required'. The following summer there was the innovation of an 8.55 pm mixed train from Haughley to Laxfield on Saturdays, a goods working leaving Laxfield at 7 pm providing the locomotive; it did not last long.

By this time most fare concessions had been abolished. The Tuesday market fare was available by the second up train alone to third class passengers only, and in 1922 it was replaced by cheap day returns at four-thirds the single fare on Tuesdays to Ipswich and on Thursdays to Stowmarket. These were soon followed, possibly through Mr Parker's influence and Great Eastern connections, by weekend returns between Mid-Suffolk and GER stations at the same rate (a minimum of 5s. was charged, with fractions of 3d. counting as 3d.). On Saturdays cheap days and half-day tickets were available to Haughley, and in summer excursion tickets were available to stations throughout East Anglia.

While traffic had held up well up to and during the war, there were signs soon after that it was starting to fall off. The extent to which that process gathered speed can be judged from the MSLR receipts book for all traffic for June 1921, which bears alarming comparison with the entry for October 1908 (*see page 37*). Showing how the line was increasingly dependent on traffic between its two ends and particularly funnelling onto it at Haughley, it read:

	£	s.	d.	%
Haughley	52	19	6	42
Mendlesham	5	11	0½	5
Aspall	7	19	6	7
Kenton	6	19	8½	6
Stradbroke	20	15	5½	16
Laxfield	29	2	5½	24
	£123	7	8	

Back in 1904 Mr Gillingwater had told the MSLR Board that a passenger and freight service could be operated for £35 a week; by now even that would result in a loss. The only mitigating factor is that it is misleading to compare June, without beet traffic and with little coal, with October. But the total running costs for 1921 came to £19,338, against receipts of £14,087.

By now the passage of the 1921 Railways Act, which brought about the 'grouping' of almost all mainland Britain's railways into the 'Big Four' companies, made the end of the line's independent existence a near certainty. It is possible to argue that the takeover of the Mid-Suffolk by the London and North Eastern Railway saved it from a quicker end, but the immediate concern of the company's creditors was to get at least some of their money back. At the same time the LNER was well aware of the company's massive debts, and saw no reason why it should have to accept responsibility for them when the creditors should have all but given up hope of getting anything. The upshot was that a wrangle over the terms of the takeover developed which prevented the merger taking place on the first day of 1924 as intended. At this point the Railways Amalgamation Tribunal, its task otherwise at an end apart from the equally insolvent Leek and Manifold line in Staffordshire, packed the case off to the Court of Appeal for a final decision. 'However the Act is applied', the

MID-SUFFOLK LIGHT RAILWAY

TIME TABLE.

July 12th, 1920, and until further notice.

This Time Table is only intended to fix the time at which Passengers may obtain their tickets for any journey from the various stations, it being understood that the Trains shall not start from them before the appointed time, but notice is hereby given, that the Company do not undertake that the trains shall start or arrive at the time specified in the table, nor will they be accountable for any loss, inconvenience or injury which may arise from delays or detentions, unless upon proof that such loss, inconvenience, injury, delay, or detention arose in consequence of the wilful misconduct of the Company's Servants. The Company do not hold themselves responsible for the correctness of the times over other Company's lines, nor the arrival of this Company's own trains in time for the nominally corresponding Train of any other Company. Passengers booking at intermediate stations can only do so conditionally upon there being room in the Train.

On Bank Holidays and exceptional occasions the Train Service shewn in the Time Tables is subject to alteration. Particulars will be obtainable at the Stations.

UP TRAINS.	Week Days.		Sundays.	DOWN TRAINS.	Week Days.		Sundays.
	a.m. p.m.	p.m.	p.m.		a.m. a.m.	p.m.	p.m.
Laxfield ....dep.	8.15 1. 0	3.25	5.30	London (L'pool St.) dep.	5. 0 10.12	3.10	4.25
Wilby .... —	8.23 1. 8	3.33	5.38	Colchester .... „	7.40 11.34	3.33	5.40
Stradbroke .... —	8.28 1.13	3.40	5.43	Felixstowe (Town) ... „	8. 0 11. 6	3.31	5. 5
Horham .... —	8.33 1.18	3.47	5.47	Ipswich .... „	9.25 12. 7	4.50	6.22
Worlingworth ... —	8.39 1.25	3.54	5.53	Stowmarket .... „	9.53 12.35	5.16	6.50
Kenton .... —	8.46 1.37	4. 3	6. 1	Haughley—G.E.R. ... arr.	9.59 12.43	5.24	6.58
Aspall & Thorndon	8.53 1.44	4.15	6. 6				
(For Debenham)				Norwich (Thorpe) ... dep.	8.51 10.22	3.44	5.54
Brockford & Wetheringsett	9. 0 1.53	4.22	6.14	Diss .... „	9.33 11.14	4.39	7. 3
Mendlesham ...... —	9. 6 2. 0	4.28	6.19	Haughley—G.E.R. ... arr.	9.52 11.41	5. 8	7.30
Haughley ...,.......arr.	9.19 2.15	4.42	6.32				
				Peterborough........... dep.	... 9.48	1. 5	2.33
Haughley—G.E.R. ... dep.	10. 2 3.10	5.12	9.14	March .... „	... 10.19	1.51	3.55
Bury St. Edmunds ... arr.	10.25 3.33	5.35	9.37	Ely .... „	... 10.52	2.30	4.32
Cambridge .... „	12.35 5.13	6.56	....	Cambridge .... „	7.11 10.59	1.35	5. 2
Ely .... „	12.26 5. 5	7.36 A	...	Bury St. Edmunds ... dep.	8.30 12.25	3.32B	6.15
March .... „	12.54 7. 2	8.20 A	...	Haughley—G.E.R. ... arr.	8.54 12.49	3.56B	6.39
Peterborough .... „	1.35 7.28	8.57 A	...				
				Haughley ....dep.	10. 5 12.55	5.30	7.34
Haughley—G.E.R. ... dep.	9.34 2.59	5.24	6.58	Mendlesham........—	10.18 1. 9	5.44	7.48
Diss .... arr.	9.58 3.24	5.50	7.23	Brockford & Wetheringsett	10.24 1.16	5.49	7.53
Norwich (Thorpe) „	10.46 4.13	6.29	8.14	Aspall & Thorndon ...—	10.32 1.25	5.57	8. 1
				(For Debenham)			
Haughley—G.E.R. ... dep.	9.52 2.40	5. 8	6.40	Kenton ....—	10.37 1.35	6. 2	8. 6
Stowmarket............ arr.	9.58 2.47	5.15	6.46	Worlingworth......—	10.45 1.42	6.13	8.14
Ipswich .... „	10.17 3. 3	5.43	7.11	Horham ....—	10.55 1.48	6.19	8.20
Felixstowe (Town)... „	11. 0 4.58	7. 6	9.14	Stradbroke ....—	11. 0 1.53	6.23	8.24
Colchester .... „	10.58 4. 5	6.36	8.42	Wilby ....—	11. 5 1.58	6.28	8.29
London (L'pool St.) „	12.39 4.58	7.52	9.10	Laxfield ....arr.	11.15 2. 5	6.35	8.36

NOTES.

A Via Cambridge.

B On Wednesdays leaves Bury at 4.10 and arrives at Haughley 4.34 p.m.

Children under 3 years, Free; above 3 and under 12, Half-fare.

MARKET TICKETS.

On Tuesdays Third Class Market Tickets, available for return on the same day, are issued at a Single Fare and a Half to Haughley from all Stations by the first and second up trains, and

On Thursdays by the second up train only.

CONVEYANCES.

Passengers may be able to arrange with the following for conveyances to meet the trains:

MENDLESHAM—P. Clements, Back Street.

BROCKFORD & WETHERINGSETT—G. Lockwood, Brockford.

ASPALL & THORNDON (Debenham)—J. Bull, Debenham.

KENTON—W. Everson, The Laurels.

WORLINGWORTH—Horse Vehicles—T. Whatling, Farmer. Motors—A. J. Pipe, near The Church.

HORHAM—J. Whatling, Farmer.

STRADBROKE—W. T. Debenham & Son, Cartage Agents.

WILBY—S. Whatling, Stradbroke.

LAXFIELD—Horse Vehicles—A. Moss, Cartage Agent. Motors—Grayston Brothers, Station Road.

For Particulars of Rates for Parcels, Merchandise, Coal, &c., and other information apply to the Station Masters, or to

W. LINDSEY-BADCOCK,

General Superintendent, LAXFIELD.

G5-4468.   100 C 600 P

J. Nawas, Printer, Stowmarket.

Timetable bill from 1920.   *Public Record Office*

Railway Magazine observed dryly at the time, 'it is difficult to avoid apparent injustice to one or other of the parties concerned'.

The Court of Appeal duly sided with the LNER's argument that the debenture holders, who were holding out for full reimbursement plus interest, were looking a gift horse in the mouth. But the new company was unwilling to face an appeal to the House of Lords that would swallow up months' if not years' receipts from the line, so set its chief legal adviser, Mr R. Francis Dunnell, to negotiate privately with debenture holders and creditors. There were claims from the insurance companies who held the largest debenture stakes and from Mr E.H. Smith, the Mid-Suffolk's solicitor since the outset, who had acquired £7,000 worth. There were also the sums owed to present and former members of the Board: £5,017 to the Earl of Stradbroke, £3,666 to Mr Remnant and £3,590 to Mr Cobbold. Mr Dunnell estimated the total liabilities, including £10,000 in unpaid debenture interest, at £89,794 - but by astute negotiation managed to buy them out for £29,960. Almost half of this, £13,060, went to the Eagle Star as it was now known; the Earl got £460, and Messrs Remnant and Cobbold £360 each.

It also turned out that the Mid-Suffolk company had been paid £5,428 more in subsidies by the Ministry of Transport than Whitehall later felt it should have had; citing an 'excess of maintenance', the Ministry asked the LNER to repay the money and was eventually satisfied with £2,000. The Mid-Suffolk eventually appeared on the new company's books at a value of £30,231 - £28,161 for land, track and property, and £1,615 for its rolling stock. This compares with just over £200,000 spent by the company in constructing and fitting out the line.

The 'Middy's' independent existence finally ended on 1st July, 1924 when the LNER officially took charge. It was rumoured locally that the line's survival was the result of Lord Huntingfield, Conservative MP for Eye, having taken the Parliamentary committee responsible for such matters out to an exceptionally good lunch; maybe he intervened with some of the debenture holders to accept Mr Dunnell's terms, which were particularly tough on the Mid-Suffolk Directors.

Having been reluctant to take the line over in the first place, the LNER lost little time in putting its stamp on the Mid-Suffolk, while at the same time allowing its own 'little ways' to continue. For a start the new company, despite having taken the Mid-Suffolk's locomotives into stock, speedily exiled them and brought in tank engines of its own preferred type: the 'Blackwall Tanks' which the Great Eastern had lent ever more often during and after the war to cover for breakdowns on the branch. As has been mentioned, they had difficulty getting up Haughley Bank but were to stay for almost a quarter of a century. Former Great Eastern carriages were also brought in to replace the MSLR's own second-hand stock. A couple of miles of the worst track were relaid with bullhead rail, but for 15 years trains from Laxfield continued to use the Mid-Suffolk's own terminus at Haughley. The standard LNER fares structure was also applied.

The most obvious economy measure instituted by the new management was the retirement of the seven crossing-keepers; after this, train crews did the job, with, at each place, the fireman ready to open the gates for the train to pass through and the guard prepared to close them before it restarted . . . in places letting schoolchildren do it for a penny a time. While no major accident took place thereafter, there were occasions when one of the nearly 120 crossings was occupied or one with gates was left open when a train came and the inevitable happened. In time the line gained a reputation for such incidents, and the number of gated crossings - 11 were still safely in the hands of station staff - was reduced by attrition.

Train services changed little, this timetable for 1924 being typical of the period. Two locomotives were in steam with a third (initially) in reserve, with one duty unchanged throughout the week and the other markedly different on Tuesdays:

Duty A (Weekdays)

	11.05	am	ex-Laxfield	mixed	*arr.* Haughley	12.10 pm
	1.00	pm	ex-Haughley	mixed	*arr.* Laxfield	2.05 pm
	3.25	pm	ex-Laxfield	passenger	*arr.* Haughley	4.40 pm
SX	5.40	pm	ex-Haughley	passenger	*arr.* Laxfield	6.45 pm
SO	6.05	pm	ex-Haughley	passenger	*arr.* Laxfield	7.10 pm

Duty B (TuX)

	7.35	am	ex-Laxfield	mixed	*arr.* Haughley	8.40 am
	9.40	am	ex-Haughley	mixed	*arr.* Laxfield	10.45 am
	12.00	noon	ex-Laxfield	freight	to Aspall	
	2.55	pm	ex-Aspall*	freight	to Laxfield	

Duty C (TuO)

	3.55	am	ex-Laxfield	cattle/freight	to Haughley	
	6.15	am	ex-Haughley	freight	to Laxfield	
	8.10	am	ex-Laxfield	mixed	*arr.* Haughley	9.15 am
	9.40	am	ex-Haughley	mixed	*arr.* Laxfield	10.45 am

* Haughley if required.

HAUGHLEY TO LAXFIELD BRANCH.

This branch is worked with a split train staff for each of the two sections, but no tickets.

Kenton is a staff crossing place and the complete train staff or one or other half thereof for the section concerned must be carried by each train when travelling over this single line.

A train conveying the ticket staff is subject to the same instructions as apply to a train conveying a ticket.

When a train is ready to start from a station and no second train is intended to follow before the staff will be required for a train in the opposite direction, the person in charge of the staff working must give the complete train staff to the driver of the train before it proceeds through the single line section concerned. If another train is intended to follow the first train before the staff can be returned, the staff must be divided and the driver of the first train given the ticket half of the staff and the driver of the second train given the other half of the staff.

On arrival at the other end of the section of both trains, the person in charge of the staff working must screw the ticket staff into the staff and lock it with the lock and key provided.

A train carrying the train staff only must not be allowed to follow a train conveying the ticket staff until the person in charge has ascertained by telephone that the preceding train has passed out of the section.

An extract appertaining to the railway from the LNER Appendix to the Working Timetable of 17th October, 1927.

The 9.40 am mixed train from Haughley was re-timed on Tuesdays first to 9.48 and then to 9.45, and the 8.10 am from Laxfield which balanced it to 8.05, allowing more time for shunting and connections at Haughley. On occasion extra freight trains were run, usually immediately after a scheduled passenger train which would sport at its rear a circular red board with a black letter 'P' to alert crossing keepers to expect a 'special'. Nine or ten goods vehicles plus a guard's van would generally be attached to mixed trains; the first train of the day to Haughley also carried a through milk van to Bishopsgate. There had always been a considerable influx of Great Eastern wagons onto the line and after the grouping the Mid-Suffolk's own limited stock was steadily diluted.

It was during the 1920s that the line began to suffer heavily from bus competition, especially on routes serving Mendlesham and Stradbroke, and to a lesser extent Laxfield. The growth of car ownership also began to eat into passenger revenue; the prospect of a slow cross-country journey punctuated by shunting before the main line was even reached was not an incentive to travel, the more so as most stations were well away from the villages they set out to serve. More worryingly still, local farm produce began to be carried by lorry, with short-haul traffic in particular enticed away from the less convenient railway.

Nevertheless it was freight and parcels traffic that kept the line in business. By 1930 passenger receipts totalled only £990 for the entire year out of £8,337; twice as much was taken for parcels as for passengers. The line was still making an operating surplus of £1,471. The outward freight traffic in sugar beet was stable, but shipments of farm produce direct to London were falling off. Cattle traffic for Ipswich was slowing to the point where the special Tuesday timetable had been abandoned by the outbreak of World War II. Inward traffic consisted of mixed freight from Ipswich and Felixstowe docks, coal from Midlands collieries and roadstone from sidings at Wymondham, Leicestershire, where the line from St Pancras to Nottingham via Oakham joined the Midland and Great Northern. (This pattern of trade underlines the Great Eastern's earlier suspicions about the MSLR and the Midland.) In 1930 59,978 tons of freight were handled, and 577 wagons of livestock.

However all this traffic fell sharply as the depression set in, and by 1933 the LNER management was looking seriously at the possibility of closure; it had already raised some cash by starting to sell off the trackbed of the Debenham branch to local farmers in 1931/32, though it was to be 1966 before the last parcel was disposed of. What the LNER had in mind was not simply abandoning the line but converting it into a road running from Laxfield to exchange sidings at Haughley. A scheme was drawn up and carefully costed; the problem was that the trackbed would be out of commission for a year, the road would cost £219,828 to build - more than the railway had - and much of the traffic now using the railway would switch to other railheads or make its entire journey by road. The Eastern Counties bus company, which was now also losing passengers, would have to be subsidised to run a replacement bus service and the entire venture, it was concluded, would involve the LNER in a heavy annual loss. Thus the line was reprieved, a 10-year track renewal begun in 1934, though left incomplete by the outbreak of war, and eventually the long-overdue rationalisation at Haughley put into effect.

MID-SUFFOLK LIGHT RAILWAY

HAUGHLEY and LAXFIELD—Week Days only.											
Mls	**Down.**	mrn	mrn	aft	aft	**Mls**	**Up.**	mrn	mrn	aft	
	856 London (L'pool St) dep	5 30	10 3	3 10	3 40	2½	Laxfield ....dep	25 11 3		3 25	
—	Haughley ....dep	9 38	1 0	5 30	6 5	2½	Willby	7 33 1111		3 33	
4½	Mendlesham ....|sett	9 51	1 13	5 43	6 18	4	Stradbroke............ ...	7 38 1116		3 38	
6	Brockford and Wetherling	10 2	1 29	5 52	6 27	5	Horham	7 43 1121		3 45	
8½	Aspall and Thorndon F.	1010	1 40	6 0	6 35	7	Worlingworth	7 49 1127		3 51	
10	Kenton	1019	1 45	6 5	6 40	9	Kenton....................	7 56 1134		3 58	
12	Worlingworth	1031	1 56	6 16	6 51	10½	Aspall & Thorndon F..|sett	8 4 1141		4 10	
14	Horham.....................	1037	2 2	6 22	6 57	13	Brockford and Wetherling	8 12 1152		4 19	
15	Stradbroke	1042	2 7	6 27	7 2	14½	Mendlesham.....|876, 877	8 25 12 9		4 30	
16½	Willby	1047	2 12	6 32	7 7	19	Haughley £56, 858, arr	8 42 1224		4 54	
19	Laxfield .... arr	1054	2 19	6 39	7 14	102	858 London (L'pool St) arr	1115,3 42		7 52	

Timetable from Bradshaw for March 1938.

Even at the close of the 1930s with war clouds gathering, all hope not only of long term survival but even of extension had not yet gone. On 3rd August, 1939, Mr Edgar Granville, Liberal MP for Eye for much of the line's life and eventually a Labour life peer, asked the Minister of Transport if he would consider asking the LNER to 'complete the unfinished portion of the line in order to provide increased direct transport facilities in an area where road communication did not achieve that purpose'. The Minister, Captain Euan Wallace, replied that powers for construction had expired 27 years previously, and that fresh authority would have to be obtained.

The outbreak of war the following month gave the line added purpose, whatever its long term future. The LNER management toyed briefly with the idea of halting passenger services, but petrol rationing and cuts in bus services increased its value to the local community and some evacuees were brought on it from the cities, and in October 1939 a reduced emergency timetable took effect for the duration of hostilities - and as chance would have it for the rest of the line's existence. The number of passenger-carrying trains was finally cut to two daily, leaving Laxfield at 7.25 am and 2.30 pm and returning from Haughley - from now on the bay platform at the main line station - at 11.00 am and 4.50 pm. Only one of the branch's tank engines engine was in use for much of the time and the journey times were increased, the 11.00 from Haughley taking two hours for the 19 miles. Extra unscheduled summer evening trains connecting with services from Liverpool Street also became a thing of the past with the outbreak of war.

It was on the freight side that the impact of war on the branch was most evident. Air bases at Mendlesham and Horham eventually operated by the Americans relied on the railway to an extent for the transport of asphalt from Haughley for construction, equipment and munitions, the Mendlesham air base generating the bulk of the traffic. To cope with this, the LNER constructed new exchange sidings at Haughley on the site of the MSLR station, with heavy freight locomotives venturing over Haugh Lane bridge and onto the foot of Haughley Bank for shunting, the first quarter-mile being strengthened. By 1943 tender engines were using the branch for the first time as 'J15' 0-6-0s, banked out of Haughley by heavier locomotives, handled the military traffic at least to Gipping and often beyond; however special goods trains were infrequent, most ammunition trucks being attached to scheduled services.

Wagons carrying high explosive were sometimes parked at Gipping until they could be taken for rapid unloading to Mendlesham or Horham. One hopes there were none in the siding on the day in 1944 when a 'Liberator' took off from Mendlesham for a sortie over occupied Europe, failed to gain height with its full complement of bombs, and crash-landed close to the railway at Gipping, its nose slithering almost onto the permanent way. Had the two explosive cargoes ignited, not only the line but several human lives even in this remote spot might have come to a premature end.

As hostilities neared their close, LNER management relaxed the frustratingly over-generous timings provided for in the wartime schedules. With the return of peace, passenger/mixed journeys were shortened further but the service stayed limited to two return workings a day. By the winter 1946/47 timetable the following trains were scheduled:

7.45	am	ex-Laxfield	*arr.* Haughley	9.00	am
11.08	am	ex-Haughley	*arr.* Laxfield	12.40	pm
1.50	pm	ex-Laxfield	*arr.* Haughley	3.20	pm
3.54	pm	ex-Haughley	*arr.* Laxfield	5.09	pm

In addition there was a daily freight working leaving Laxfield at 10.15 am with a 12.45 pm arrival time at Haughley, leaving the junction at 1.30 to reach Laxfield at 3.25; in each direction the only compulsory stop was at Kenton. In addition, at least into 1948, there was a daily 'as required' freight for airfield traffic from Haughley to Mendlesham and back, setting out at 9.30 am and starting its return journey at 10.15; this was operated by the locomotive off the morning mixed train during its two hour layover before returning to Laxfield. During the big freeze and fuel crisis of early 1947, the timetable became somewhat academic; on one occasion it took a train two hours to cover the six miles between Brockford and Haughley, no snow plough being available.

The immediate post-war period showed several signs of confidence in the line on the part of LNER management. The track renewal programme suspended with the outbreak of war was resumed and in 1947 the last of the MSLR flat-bottomed rail was removed from the running lines, save for the final stretch to Laxfield Mills where the original rail spiked to the sleepers survived to the end, and on lesser used sidings notably at Kenton. The way was now clear for the replacement of the 'Blackwall Tanks' whose performance on the Mid-Suffolk, never ideal, had become steadily more erratic with cancellations or failures in service making the line even less attractive to passengers. Older but more powerful 'J15' 0-6-0s had been making occasional appearances on the line since 1943, and they now took over all services. If there was no longer any hope of extending the line, there must at least have been some confidence in its survival when, on 1st January, 1948, British Railways came into being and the Mid-Suffolk was under new ownership once again.

The contractor's locomotive *Lady Stevenson* at work in 1903 on the Debenham branch, probably close to the makeshift goods handling point where the track eventually ended.

The East Anglian

Locomotive No. 1 in maker's livery and named.   *Hudswell, Clarke*

Chapter Six

Locomotives and Rolling Stock

The first locomotive to run on Mid-Suffolk metals was a Manning, Wardle 'K' class 0-6-0 tank belonging to Jackson's, the contractor; they purchased it in 1900 and it must have begun hauling construction trains on the line in the second quarter of 1902. Built in 1890 and bearing the maker's number 1134, it weighed 16½ tons, had 3 ft 1⅛ in. driving wheels and cylinders 12 in. by 17 in. wide. It was owned originally by Logan and Hemingway of Beighton, near Sheffield, who gave it the number 11 and used it on construction of the Chesterfield section of the Lancashire, Derbyshire and East Coast Railway (later Great Central), and passed first to Naylor Brothers, contractors, of Ashbourne, and thence to Jackson's, who kept it on the Mid-Suffolk for a time after the arrival of *Lady Stevenson*. The contractor took it on to the Weston, Clevedon and Portishead Railway (WC&PLR), where it was used in constructing the extension from Clevedon to Portishead, and in 1907 it passed into the stock of the WC&PLR; they numbered it '2' and named it *Portishead*, the second of three engines to bear the title, possibly to mark its hauling of the first scheduled train to that town. The WC&PLR kept it until 1926, when it was sold to Wm Cowlin of Bristol, who used it on construction work on the new Portishead power station; it was cut up in the early 1930s.

As the pace of construction accelerated, Jackson's bought a second 0-6-0 tank engine direct from Manning, Wardle: one of the slightly less basic 'L' class, bearing the maker's number 1570. It was heavier and slightly more powerful than its counterpart, weighing 19 tons 18 cwt, with 3 ft driving wheels and cylinders at 12 in. by 18 in. Outshopped in March 1903, the locomotive was delivered to the line bearing the number '7' on a cast plate; it soon acquired the name *Lady Stevenson* after the Mid-Suffolk Chairman's mother, whose fortune was being lost in the promotion of the line. *Lady Stevenson* worked for Jackson's over the entire system as constructed, from Haughley and later Kenton where it was shedded, down to Debenham and probably as far as Cratfield. And when the line opened for freight in September 1904 before the arrival of the locomotives the Mid-Suffolk company had ordered, she hauled the daily goods train for the best part of three months before help arrived and she was relegated to less taxing duties. She was still owned by Jackson's, and after the Mid-Suffolk Board dismissed them in September 1905, stayed in store at Haughley until the contractor's affairs had been sorted out. Then she was sold on to the Bettisfield Colliery Co. in North Wales.

The seal of the Mid-Suffolk company depicted an 0-4-2 tank engine, but no locomotive with that wheel arrangement ever ran on the line. The Board at the outset planned to have one or perhaps two locomotives and a steam railcar, but public statements were not backed up by orders. In the event orders were placed in 1903 with Hudswell, Clarke of Leeds for two 0-6-0 side tank engines of the type already supplied to the Manchester Ship Canal, one for delivery as soon as possible and the second once the branch was opened; the maker's

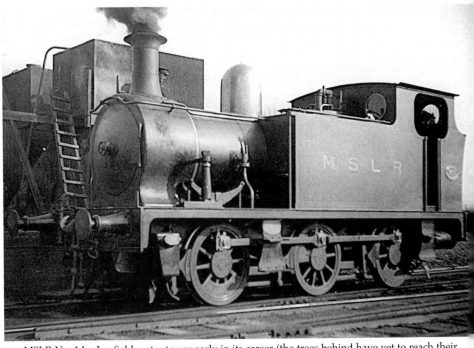

MSLR No. 1 by Laxfield water tower early in its career (the trees behind have yet to reach their full height). *Ken Nunn Collection*

No. 2 awaiting departure from Haughley, early in its career. The sandbox above the frames is a prominent feature. *Lens of Sutton*

reluctance to release the first one until they had cash in hand has already been mentioned. Each was painted crimson lake, with the initials 'M.S.L.R.' on the tanks in gold letters, and the panels lined out in yellow and vermilion. (Later in the line's independent existence when money was tighter, they gradually turned to a dirty shade of red with a cruder lining for the panels.) They had copper-topped chimneys, and polished brass domes and safety valve covers. Each had driving wheels 3 ft 4 in. in diameter and a boiler 3 ft 2 in. in diameter and 9 ft in length, ending with a working pressure of 160 lb. per square inch. But there the similarity ended.

No. 1, maker's number 711 of 1904, was outshopped bearing the name *Haughley*, but this was painted out after the official photographs had been taken and the company's initials substituted. Priced at £1,400, it had a 12 ft wheelbase, 14 in. x 20 in. cylinders, 620 gallon tanks and weighed 29 tons 12 cwt. Originally it had a squat chimney which gave an impression of some power, but before long this was replaced by a taller one; it was fitted with spark arresters from the outset, and what those near the line quickly dubbed an 'organ whistle'.

No. 2, maker's number 723 of 1905 and delivered in the opening weeks of the year, was less powerful and normally reserved for passenger duties, having been fitted with Westinghouse air brakes. Restrictions were applied to its use on freight trains on Haughley Bank over and above those for all other locomotives, three fewer wagons being permitted to No. 2 than to the others. Named *Kenton* though it probably never bore the title in service, and priced at £1,375, it was built as a 2-4-0, though it is equally unlikely that it ever ran in this form. Its most obvious difference from the line's other engines was that it had sandboxes above, rather than below, its frames; it had an 11 ft wheelbase and 600 gallon tanks, and weighed 24 tons. In later years it boasted one further difference: a patch in the cab roof where a shotgun brought onto the footplate by driver Bennett, a poacher of repute, had accidentally discharged while the engine was in Kenton shed.

A third Hudswell, Clarke side tank was ordered as soon as approval was belatedly given for a passenger service, the need being more urgent because locomotive No. 1 was out of action for major repairs. Until it could be delivered, the Mid-Suffolk had to hire a locomotive to supplement the overworked No. 2. As a stop-gap the company rented an engine named *Emlyn* from C.D. Phillips of Newport, Monmouthshire for a few weeks at the end of 1908, and again for a short period a year later. However a substantial locomotive was needed for a longer period, so from January 1909 until mid-1910, the railway rented a further Manning, Wardle saddle tank, *Chamberlain*. There is some confusion over *Chamberlain's* identity; traditionally it was thought to have been an 0-4-0 with 3 ft driving wheels and 12 in. x 18 in. outside cylinders, built in 1873 with maker's number 439. This locomotive was built for the Bedworth Colliery and Iron Co. near Coventry, and bought by Stanley Bros when the pit closed; by 1918 it was with the contractors Topham, Jones and Railton. However Peter Paye in his comprehensive book on the Mid-Suffolk concludes that *Chamberlain* was a more recent and powerful engine, 0-6-0 No. 1663 built in 1905, with 3 ft 6 in. driving wheels, 14 in. x 20 in. driving wheels and a weight of 29 tons. This engine spent its later working life at Grassmoor Colliery near Chesterfield and was scrapped

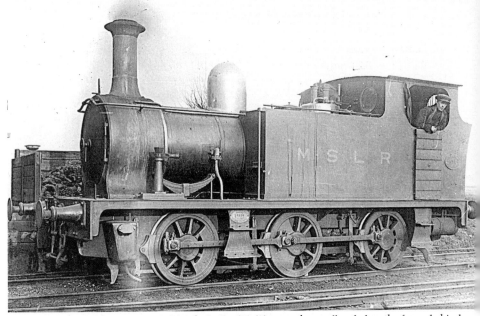

Locomotive No. 3 as it appeared for the bulk of its life; note the sandbox below the frame behind the front buffer beam, and the make-shift cab door. The exigencies of Haughley and Athelington banks, both of which were fortunately graded the same way, ensured Mid-Suffolk locomotives left Haughley facing up the branch so that the sanding gear could take effect.

H.C. Casserley Collection

Locomotive No. 3 on the scrap road at Stratford immediately after the Grouping and eviction from the branch. It never received its LNER number and was broken up within weeks.

Ken Nunn Collection

in 1935. The name, assuming it was bestowed when the locomotive was new, would make this latter suggestion the more plausible, as in 1873 Joseph Chamberlain had yet to become a national figure, while in 1905 he was nearing the end of his political career. Maybe the Manning, Wardle 0-4-0 tank was in fact *Emlyn*.

The third Mid-Suffolk locomotive, numbered 3 and supposedly named *Laxfield*, arrived from Hudswell, Clarke in April 1909 bearing the maker's number 867. Priced at £1,440, it was an 0-6-0 identical to No. 1, save that it had cast-iron wheels and a mild steel boiler. The newest locomotive ever to work on the line, it was to have a life of just 15 years.

Officially no diesel locomotive ever worked the line, which closed when steam was still king. Cliff Bloom, one of the few members of his family who did not work on the line, remembers seeing a green diesel engine standing in Mendlesham station in the 1920s. He told the MSLR Society's *Making Tracks* magazine in 1995 that 'it was about the size of an 0-6-0 steam engine, and arrived at the head of a mixed train, with the usual two coaches and some trucks. It had sand pipes at the front, and he saw it only once'. However, a Mr Pinney of Barham subsequently came forward to claim that the engine was in fact a Sentinel steam locomotive undergoing trials on the line. This apart, the contractors who lifted the line in 1953-54 did use a four-wheel diesel shunter to tow loads of track panels to a central depot at Kenton, whence a 'J15' conveyed them to Haughley.

On a humbler note, the MSLR used a petrol-engined permanent way trolley which was stationed at Brockford for duties on the section from there to Haughley; platelayers between Brockford and Laxfield had to make do with a trolley, but the inspector supervising them pedalled a 3-wheel rail-mounted 'velocipede' kept at Haughley, this was 'borrowed' on Sundays by gangers along the line to get to the pub at Mendlesham.

Just how good the MSLR engines were is a matter of dispute. The first two did not at first handle as well as expected and all required more maintenance than had been bargained for, hence the hire of *Emlyn* and *Chamberlain* and later of motive power from the Great Eastern while the Mid-Suffolk's own were under repair at Stratford. Yet their ability to tackle Haughley Bank has already been noted, and *The Locomotive* of 1st May, 1907 reported of a footplate trip on No. 1 from Laxfield to Haughley that the locomotive showed 'steady running with a comparatively heavy train'. What is certain, though, is that the GER 'brass' did not like them.

Locomotives from the 'main line' made occasional forays onto the 'Middy' from a relatively early stage with the GER weed-killer train, breakdown or ballast trains; in every recorded instance the engine in question was a Holden 'Blackwall Tank', usually from the Eye branch. So it was only a matter of time before a motive power crisis on the Mid-Suffolk brought one of them onto the line on a more formal basis. That moment came in May 1919 when No. 1 and No. 2 were both withdrawn for major repairs; the light railway company hired first GER No. 254 (LNER 7254) and later No. 157 (LNER 7157) to operate services alongside its own No. 3, staying on the line for three months. The precedent set a pattern for the future.

Bearing its new owner's name and number, if not the full livery, the former No. 1 is seen here out of service at Stratford in April 1928, five months before scrapping. It was unlikely that it ever ran again once its connecting rods had been removed. *Ken Nunn Collection*

Faring better than its two colleagues, the former No. 2 seen here in full LNER livery.
Ken Nunn Collection

With the grouping, all three Hudswell, Clarke tanks were allocated LNER numbers - 8316, 8317 and 8315 - and classified 'J64'. Yet the line's new management lost no time in getting rid of them, No. 3 hauling No. 2 to Stratford in July 1924 with No. 1 following early in August. Though the newest of the Mid-Suffolk engines and apparently the fittest, No. 3 was scrapped in the autumn of 1924 without even receiving its new number. No. 1 did a little better, receiving its new number though keeping the red Mid-Suffolk livery and working at Ipswich as a shunter until withdrawal in September 1928. The new No. 8317, though the least powerful of the three, got its full livery at Stratford in 1925 and survived a further four years - mainly shunting at Parkeston Quay - before ending its career at Colchester in December, 1929. The life of the 'J64' class had barely spanned a quarter of a century.

Onto the branch now the coast was clear came the 'Blackwall Tanks', classified 'J65' by the LNER. This class sometimes operated on branches as 2-4-0 tanks, but there is no evidence that they ever ran thus to Laxfield. First introduced in 1889, the 'J65s' had driving wheels 4 ft in diameter and cylinders 12 in. x 15 in., and weighed 27 tons 1 cwt - just lighter than two of the three Mid-Suffolk locomotives. The first 'Blackwall Tanks' to arrive in July 1924 - from Mellis - were Nos. 7153 and 7157, the latter surviving World War II and renumbering to 8212 to be scrapped, fresh from the branch, in November 1947. Among others which made up the three locomotives at Laxfield between the wars (the allocation was cut to two with the introduction of the wartime service) were Nos. 7153, 7156, 7247, 7253, 7254 and 7257. By 1946 No. 7250 was working on the line; soon to be renumbered 8214, it was as No. 68214 to be the last survivor of the class, scrapped in 1956; the final 'J65' to operate from Laxfield, in 1948, was No. 7155 (renumbered 8211).

One engine which was briefly tried on the 'Middy' was the ex-Great Central Railway 'J62' class 0-6-0 tank No. 5889. One of a class of twelve locomotives designed by Pollitt and built at Gorton in 1897. This was transferred in 1930 from its home base at Immingham for trials at Ipswich docks. No. 5889 spent a few days at the most on the line in December 1930, before being sent back to the old Great Central the following month. Renumbered 8202 in 1946, it was broken up in December 1947.

As the 'Blackwall Tanks' were withdrawn, tender engines took over, given access to the branch by the completion of the LNER's programme to relay almost all of its trackwork with bullhead rail instead of the lighter Mid-Suffolk flat-bottom, which had necessitated severe weight restrictions. (That these restrictions were justified was shown after closure in 1953 when the un-relaid siding at Laxfield Mill buckled under the lifting contractors' crane.) The outstanding obstacles to the operation of tender engines were the lack of a turntable at either end of the line (that at Haughley had been removed long since) and a restriction of 15 mph on locomotives running tender first. However 0-6-0 tender engines of the ubiquitous 'J15' class had been venturing onto the line since at least 1943 out of sheer necessity on ballast and ammunition trains, and by the end of 1947 (and of the LNER) the first of these obstacles was overcome and the second put aside as they took over the branch, being shedded at Laxfield.* The 'J15s', the last class to work the line and the oldest (except

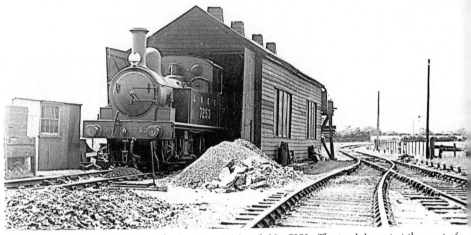

Laxfield shed in July 1936, with class 'J65' 0-6-0 tank No. 7253. The track layout at the west of the yard is clearly seen; in the distance is the Laxfield signal. *H.C. Casserley*

No. 65447 on shed at Laxfield, 1st September, 1951. Despite the loss of part of the roof in a storm, the shed is still dark enough to conceal No. 65388, steamed on only three days a week outside the sugar beet season. *H.C. Casserley*

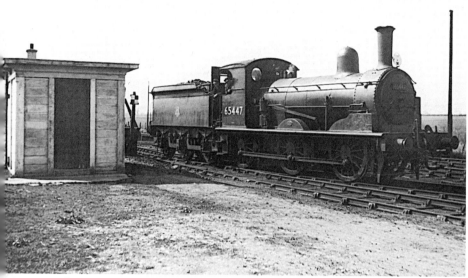

No. 65447 shunts at Laxfield, 16th April, 1952. She has just detached trucks from an incoming mixed train. *R.M. Casserley*

A close up of the controls of 'J15' class 0-6-0 No. 65447, which hauled most trains in the final years. *H.N. James*

Two of the original four-wheel coaches seen on an early mixed train at Haughley station, with locomotive No. 2 ready to depart. *Ken Nunn Collection*

The ex-GER 'cattle truck' six-wheeler coaches as delivered to Laxfield in early LNER days. *Real Photographs*

possibly for *Emlyn*), having been built from 1887, held sway on branches throughout East Anglia and right up to Liverpool Street throughout the 1940s and 1950s until almost the end of steam. Weighing 67 tons 15 cwt with tender, and with 4 ft 11 in. driving wheels and 17½ in. x 24 in. cylinders, they were ideal nevertheless for light mixed traffic work and many other duties. (The author remembers travelling behind one in 1957 from Loughton - long since the province of Tube trains alone - to Liverpool Street in a nine-coach excursion train of Gresley corridor stock bound for the South coast.) There was a stable of 'J15s' based on Ipswich shed to operate on branches throughout Suffolk including the Laxfield line. To give the crew some rudiments of protection from the elements in a cab offering little shelter, the 'J15s' on the Mid-Suffolk were often fitted with crude and easily transferable weather boards.

Nos. 65447 (replacing 65459) and 65388 performed the bulk of the duties for the final five years of the line's existence, but many other 'J15s' made occasional appearances, among them Nos. 65361, 65404, 65407, 65408, 65422, 65429, 65430, 65454, 65467, 65470 and 65471. No. 65447 distinguished itself not simply by hauling the final scheduled trains on the Mid-Suffolk but by being the last co-survivor of its class, being withdrawn in November 1962 with No. 65462, gratifyingly preserved and now on the North Norfolk Railway. While No. 65447 was fitted with Westinghouse and vacuum brakes and was thus suited for all working, No. 65388 had a steam brake only and thus could only handle the thrice-weekly freight trains. Delay in repainting the tender of No. 65447 in April 1951 led to its being temporarily paired with 'water-cart' tender No. 8892, which had been separated from 'D15' 4-4-0 No. 62503 on its withdrawal the previous February. Such pairings normally occurred only among classes 'D13', 'D15' and 'E4'; No. 65451 was the only other 0-6-0 to be so matched. Around this time, No. 65447 was also turned out by Ipswich shed with a cream interior lining to its cab; this former Great Eastern tradition was revived by several Ipswich crews in that year and No. 65447 was selected along with several main line locomotives. Cab fittings were burnished, and some exterior paintwork chipped in the process to give a glimpse of Great Eastern blue, painted over 27 years previously.

The original carriages used when passenger trains began to run in 1908 were three ex-Metropolitan Railway two-class four-wheelers, rendered surplus by electrification. Well before then four 'spares' were ready for excursion traffic, a second rake of three carriages being made up when the MSLR's third locomotive arrived in 1909. The coaches of one of the sets, each of which dated from the 1880s, had a central corridor to allow for conductor-guard operation, but little use was made of this facility despite the economies it offered at sparsely used stations. This set also had a first class saloon for Directors and privileged passengers created by knocking two compartments together; as has been mentioned, it was always turned out for the Tuesday market service. Its coaches had acetylene gas plants which had the disconcerting habit of freezing in winter; to offset this, foot-warmers were kept in readiness at Laxfield. The second set comprised three four-wheel passenger brake composites which were

---

* In 1946 a shortage of motive power led to an 'E4' 2-4-0, No. 7466 (renumbered 2782) being shedded at Laxfield. On very rare occasions in BR days, other 'E4s' are said to have been used, and also 'J69' tank engines. However 'E4s' were apparently never contemplated as an alternative to the 'J15s' on the Mid-Suffolk.

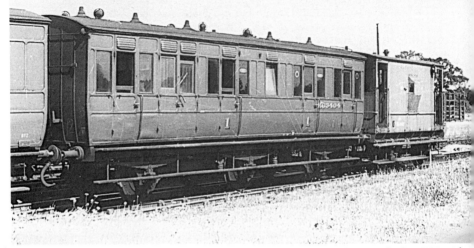

The last days of Victorian luxury: composite carriage No. E63404, built at Stratford in 1897, with two first class and three second class compartments, in a mixed train formation ready for departure from Laxfield on 1st September, 1951. It had less than four months of active service ahead of it. *H.C. Casserley*

A close-up of ex-GER brake third No. E62931 during run-round at Laxfield on 1st September, 1951. Built at Stratford in 1901, it was withdrawn the following January and broken up a month later. *H.C. Casserley*

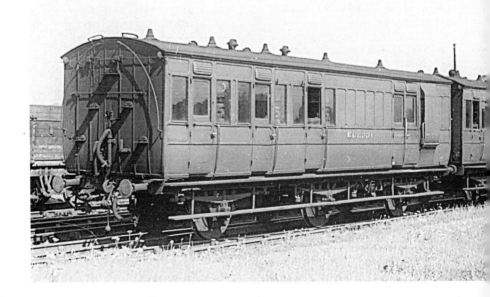

One of the Mid-Suffolk's two horse boxes at Laxfield just after delivery. *H.C. Casserley Collection*

The second goods brake, posed at the manufacturer's to show its far more sophisticated construction than No. 1. *R.W. Kidner Collection*

used in all mixed trains, and occasionally coupled to the other set on the rare occasions when traffic justified a train of six carriages. All seven ex-Metropolitan Railway coaches had been rebuilt at the Langley Mill, Notts, works of G.R. Turner and Son, whence they had been taken from Neasden; while there, their vacuum brakes were replaced by a Westinghouse system and they were painted dark brown.

The Mid-Suffolk's original coaching stock was banished from the line almost as quickly as its locomotives. Within weeks if not months of the LNER taking over in July 1924, all seven carriages were off the branch *en route* to the breakers, their place being taken by eight ex-GER six-wheelers displaced by 'Jazz' stock from North London suburban services; normally run in two-car rakes of both classes with an extra coach added if necessary, they had 'cattle-truck' partitions between the third class compartments. The most noticeable attribute of this stock was the squealing noise as it took the 'Middy's' tighter curves. The windows of each compartment were held closed by a leather strap secured over a knob on the lower window ledge; the author's grandfather, who travelled in such carriages on the way to school in the 1890s, recalled that passengers often had to travel with the windows open because the straps had been stolen to fulfil an equally practical purpose as strops to sharpen cut-throat razors. Built between 1897 and 1902, the coaches had been fully refurbished before delivery to the line, but it soon wore off: by the withdrawal of the final pair in 1951 their roofs leaked so badly that carriages from main line stopping trains had on occasion to be detached at Haughley to substitute. The Mid-Suffolk had by then become the last line on the entire British Railways' system on which non-bogie steam hauled stock was used, save for two miners' services in South Wales.

For the final nine months of the line's existence, the six-wheelers gave way to a later generation of ex-suburban stock: two pairs of bogie carriages freed for service on the branch by the Liverpool Street-Shenfield electrification which arrived in October 1951. They were fitted for push-and-pull operation with the brake van converted to a driving trailer and had at times run as such on quieter lines in the London area; even in the late 1950s after electrification, their counterparts could be found on early Sunday services from Liverpool Street to Ongar, propelled by an 'F5' 2-4-2 tank engine. However the 'J15s' were not push-and-pull fitted, so the two sets on the Mid-Suffolk were never driven from the train. By comparison with what had gone before, these carriages offered passengers a frustratingly brief taste of dryness and relative modernity, if not of luxury: although they boasted electric light which flickered during station stops, the compartments were cramped compared with those of the older stock. One curiosity of the sets, which still offered first- as well as third-class accommodation, was that in one carriage alternate compartments were partitioned only to the tops of the seat backs, offering the school children who now comprised most of the 'Middy's' passengers scope for considerable amusement. On the last day of operation, all four carriages were pressed into service, then left in a siding at Haughley. A few weeks later they were retrieved and towed to Stratford where new uses were found for them, one surviving as a van until 1966.

The line began with 30 new non-passenger vehicles from Turner's of Langley

Mill: two Westinghouse-fitted horse boxes, six cattle wagons, one box wagon, four low-sided and 14 high-sided trucks, a parcels van and two four-wheel goods brakes. On mixed trains, the trucks were always marshalled behind the carriages, with a goods brake bringing up the rear - or a passenger brake if none were available. The Mid-Suffolk's own stock could usually cope, but in the early years, cattle traffic on Ipswich market days could require up to 30 trucks; those the company could not supply itself were hired from the GER at three shillings a day. This traffic was far from popular with the drovers who at one time had herded cattle all the way to market and more recently to the Great Eastern railhead at Framlingham, for the MSLR stations to which they now delivered their charges were notoriously distant from licensed premises.

By the Grouping the company's stock was down to 21 vehicles, kept as far as possible on the branch; they were, of course, supplemented by the use of colliery companies' own trucks for incoming coal traffic. When the LNER introduced through running, trucks came in at random, but they still had to be shunted through the exchange sidings. There were some kept on the branch for local use, apart from the van reserved for through milk traffic to London each morning. Right to the end, the line also kept two goods brakes of its own; as has been mentioned, great efforts were made in shunting at Kenton to make sure each returned to its 'own' end of the line. In the late 1940s one van failed and was left at Haughley just as a totally refurbished brake for a new prestige goods service was detached from a train there *en route* for Parkeston Quay. Peter Paye tells how the next Mid-Suffolk train made off with this sparkling vehicle, leaving the authorities baffled as to where it had gone until, months later, a BR traffic inspector found it at Laxfield being used as a greenhouse by the station porter.

A rare view of the MSLR's first goods brake, with an open wagon. *R.W. Kidner Collection*

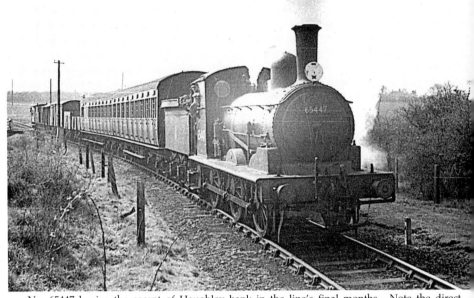

No. 65447 begins the ascent of Haughley bank in the line's final months. Note the direct connection from the main line at the rear of the train. *H.N. James*

No. 65447, oozing steam in a disconcerting number of places, heads a Laxfield train through the cutting between Mendlesham and Brockford. The bridge carrying the A140 Ipswich-Norwich road can just be seen in the distance. *H.N. James*

Chapter Seven

Indian Summer and Closure

Britain's railways passed into public ownership at just the point when the boost to traffic provided by war was subsiding, the public turning to other modes of travel despite the continuing austerity. The Mid-Suffolk was not well placed to compete, passing through a relatively thinly populated area across, rather than along, natural lines of communication, and with services slowed severely by speed restrictions, shunting and the increasing need to open and close level crossing gates *en route*. In the event, it was to survive as part of British Railways for just over four and a half years.

Nationalisation as such had no tangible impact on the line, save for the renumbering and re-lettering of locomotives when they next went in for overhaul. But it did coincide almost exactly with two changes of note: the arrival a few weeks before 'vesting day' of tender engines to replace the long-serving 'Blackwall Tanks', and the first (and only) through working onto the main system in the history of the line. This involved the 4.42 pm from Haughley to Laxfield on Mondays to Fridays beginning its journey at Stowmarket to pick up school children for stations along the branch; the manoeuvres at Haughley to gain access to the Mid-Suffolk, despite the installation of a direct connection, have already been described.

Services in the line's final years remained very much on the wartime pattern. Trains left Laxfield at 7.21 am and 1.45 pm (the earliest 'last train' since the first months of passenger service), returning from Haughley at 11.15 am, 3.55 pm (SO), and 4.42 pm (SX, starting from Stowmarket). By 1951 only the morning trains were mixed, generally with four or five freight wagons. There was also a special freight working on Mondays, Wednesdays and Fridays which left Laxfield at 10.15 am, reaching Haughley at 12.45 pm and returning at 1.30 pm. Even outside the sugar beet season when this train ran daily until the end, this took more wagons than the daily mixed trains. The short working from Haughley to Mendlesham and back officially ceased in 1950.

Passenger traffic, always light, fell off more sharply than freight as prosperity and car ownership grew. Increasingly often, the 11.15 am from Haughley and the return 1.45 pm from Laxfield ran without a single passenger. Proof was offered in the process that for passenger-only trains, the times allowed were laughably generous despite the need to stop ever more often for unmanned road crossings. On Saturdays the 3.55 pm from Haughley would pull steadily ahead of time to reach Laxfield 20 minutes or more early, so that its Ipswich crew could cycle furiously to catch a homeward connection on the East Suffolk line. They felt no need to observe the timetable as the line's only remaining adult season ticket holder, from Kenton to Laxfield, never travelled on Saturdays and they did not expect anyone else to appear. On one occasion they were in too much of a hurry for their own good, leaving the guard behind at Wilby and having to go back for him.

While the relaid track was in good condition and different, if still aged,

No. 65447 occupies the first few yards of the Laxfield Mills extension after bringing in the 11.15 am from Haughley on 16th April, 1952. The arrival on the line of ex-LNER suburban bogie stock forced trains to pull further up the tiny platform at Laxfield with the first carriage, and not just the engine as before, blocking the level crossing. *R.M. Casserley*

No. 65447's fireman opens a crossing gate on one of the line's more remote and overgrown sections for his Haughley-bound passenger train in the final month of operation. *H.N. James*

locomotives had been brought in, there were other signs of decay. The engine shed at Laxfield lost much of its roof in a storm in 1951 and no effort was made to restore it, and that autumn the line's leaky coaching stock was condemned and replaced by relatively recent, if spartan, bogie carriages. All the time, mishaps at level crossings were reducing the number of gates - pieces of rope with a red flag attached substituted for those which had come to grief, as at Worlingworth in 1951. The attrition of crossing gates was bad news for local schoolchildren who were often given a penny by the train crew to open and shut them. On a more serious note, it was in the final years of the line's operation with services pared to a minimum that the second recorded fatality took place, at Brown Street - like the first four decades previously, it involved a pedestrian run down at an ungated crossing.

During the line's 'Indian summer' it attracted increasing attention both from enthusiasts and from railway management anxious to see the phenomenon at first hand; while few significant closures had taken place since the war and nationalisation, there was little doubt that the axe would fall and that it was only a matter of time before such picturesque and at times hair-raising lines as the 'Middy' became prime candidates. Branch line closures in the area were not unprecedented: the Southwold Railway with which the Mid-Suffolk had tried to entangle itself had succumbed to road competition as early as 1929 and the branch to Eye lost its passenger service two years later. It was 1951 before railway management turned its attention to the thinning out of East Anglia's unremunerative branch lines, starting with the closure of the light railway to Tollesbury in Essex, and 1952 was to mark the end for no fewer than seven lines in the region . . . among them the Mid-Suffolk. The line between Bishops Stortford and Braintree went first, on 3rd March; the Heacham-Wells branch on 2nd June; the Elsenham-Thaxted and County School-Wroxham branches on 15th September; the Framlingham line - except for the 'Fram Flyer' boarding school specials, on 1st November; and the Beccles-Tivetshall route along the Waveney Valley, comprising the northern side of the 'box' served by the Mid-Suffolk, on 29th December. All of these except the Thaxted branch and a section of the County School-Wroxham line continued for a time to handle freight. But for the Mid-Suffolk, scheduled for closure on the 28th July, the end was to be total. Born in the final months of Queen Victoria's reign, it would be laid to rest at the dawn of the new Elizabethan era.

In November 1951, just weeks after the 'new' stock arrived, the unions were notified that closure of the line was planned, and the following month formal notice was given. Needless to say, the announcement brought strong local opposition: objections were lodged by East Suffolk County Council and Hartismere rural council, and on 12th February, 1952 a public hearing was held in London. For the Railway Executive, Mr A.J. Johnson argued that the line's only significant users were around 50 schoolchildren bound for Stowmarket and farmers shipping out sugar beet, three-quarters of whom sent their produce by road in any case. The councils responded that closure would deprive a large rural area of public transport, and that farmers had shifted much of the beet traffic to lorries because of uncertainty about the line's future. But the objectors could not offset the evidence of years of virtually empty trains, and their

No. 65447 starts the climb out of Haughley from the bay platform with the morning mixed train to Laxfield. *H.N. James*

The afternoon school train from Stowmarket, headed by No. 65467, takes the crossover to the branch at Haughley. The presence of the grain silo means that the end is just months away. *Dr Ian C. Allen*

appeals were brushed aside. The Transport Users' Consultative Committee acquiesced in the closure, and after a fact finding visit by railway officials in the Norwich inspection saloon (accompanied by Dr Allen whose account of the goings on at the jammed Kenton signal on a less prominent management visit have been mentioned) complete closure of the 'Middy' was set for Monday 28th July. Final services were to run the previous Saturday; officially the line was still open the following day, but no Sunday trains had run since 1921. Given the recent renewal of the track and the still-heavy seasonal sugar beet traffic, it is a little surprising that the line did not stay open for goods traffic even through that autumn. But management had clearly concluded that the Mid-Suffolk was a hopeless case; maybe it also hoped that some of the traffic would be tapped by the railheads at Eye and Framlingham which were to survive for another decade. Sugar beet apart, freight traffic by now was light, hardly any being carried on mixed trains. But the final scheduled goods train on the Friday ran to more than a dozen trucks, plus the Laxfield water carrier and a brake van.

Just before closure, the line had a chance of lasting fame on celluloid. The classic film *The Titfield Thunderbolt* was about to be made and the company surveyed various picturesque and moribund branch lines with a view to their being chosen as the location. Early in 1952 the film-makers ran their rule over the Mid-Suffolk, but the line was not quite what they were looking for despite its idiosyncratic ways, and immortality went instead to the already closed Camerton and Limpley Stoke line south of Bath.

Yet the 'Middy' in its last days also inspired a book whose serialisation would entrance BBC television audiences four decades later and, incidentally, rekindle interest in the line. John Hadfield's *Love on a Branch Line* is more about love - or rather a heady sexual liberation - than about branch lines, being the story of Jasper Pye, a naive and earnest civil servant sent to Suffolk in the 1950s to close a government establishment which has outlived its usefulness who is caught in a fancy-free time warp. To quote the publishers' blurb, 'Arcady, the country seat of Lord Flamborough, where the ministry has its offices, is inhabited by a glorious host of eccentrics, while Lord Flamborough himself resides in a private railway train where he listens to jazz and mixes cocktails. His three daughters - Chloe, Belinda and Matilda - are all blissfully free of inhibitions, which has a liberating effect on the rather stuffy Mr Pye'. That private train was based on a line the author readily acknowledged was the Mid-Suffolk, which captivated him when he moved into the area just weeks before the last train ran. This 'sad event' inspired Mr Hadfield, already a best-selling writer, to learn all he could both about the line and the country it ran through, and in 1959 *Love on a Branch Line* was published. Much of the railway 'colour' was the author's invention, such as the tale of how Lord Flamborough had lost both his legs when the engine he had volunteered to drive during the General Strike had its brake released by strikers at Norwich. Yet his fictitious branch line, 'closed down four years ago' though His Lordship's train carried on using it and the booking clerk at Liverpool Street could mysteriously issue Jasper Pye with a ticket, ran from Arcady to a place called Flaxfield 58 minutes' journey away . . . and Flaxfield Junction is made to sound a little like Haughley prior to 1939, when the separate MSLR station was dispensed with.

No. 65447 shows a very rusty cab side as driver Ernest Baker (*left*) poses with his fireman and an imposing railway official on the platform at Haughley, 16th April, 1952. If the impending departure was the second and final train of the day, Mr Baker faced a spartan night ahead in the 'hut' at Laxfield. *R.M. Casserley*

Dr Ian C. Allen joins driver Joe Skinner on the footplate of No. 65447 as it pauses at Mendlesham with a Haughley-bound passenger train. *H.N. James*

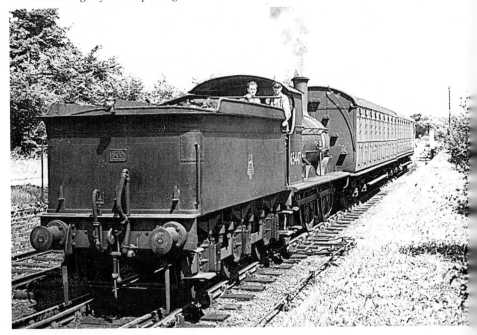

At Flaxfield Junction, as though to mark the distinction between British Railways and the Earl of Flamborough's Folly, the branch line terminated abruptly in a high corrugated iron fence which had been thrown across the rails some fifty yards from the station platform.

As befitted a work of fiction, the train announcements at the junction were a touch more exotic than they had been in real life: 'Flaxfield - junction for London, Glasgow and Kings Lynn!' Yet the train - three coaches, including a Pullman, coupled to an ancient class 'E4' Great Eastern 2-4-0 - interrupted its journeys at a halt that could only have been a typical Mid-Suffolk station:

The platform was only some fifty yards long, but there was all the usual station equipment - verandah roof with fretted edge, a bench, hanging oil lamps, a door marked 'Waiting Room', and a few tattered timetables. A single rail track curved out of sight.

Lord Flamborough told Pye he had bought the line on its closure, been presented by the railway with the locomotive which had run on the Mildenhall branch, and had had the carriages brought down from Palmers Green in the 'confusion' of a national railway strike; union members had organised the movement after his Lordship threatened to go on television and say what had happened at Norwich.

Very decent about it, they were. Cleaned the coaches and oiled round the engine before they went. And elected me Vice-President of the Flaxfield branch of the Union.

When first published, *Love on a Branch Line* achieved a moderate success and enhanced its author's literary reputation. Yet it was not to be brought to a wider audience until 1994 - by which time Brockford station had already been re-created with John Hadfield, now living at Woodbridge, taking an approving interest.

The BBC's serialisation of *Love on a Branch Line,* starring Leslie Phillips as the Earl, was too ambitious a project to make use of the short stretch of track laid by then at Brockford. Requiring a fully-operational line in East Anglia, the production team settled on the North Norfolk Railway between Sheringham and Holt which had been used for a number of other BBC productions including *Hi-De-Hi!*, and this revived stretch of the Midland and Great Northern duly played a strong supporting part in the series. One golden opportunity was missed, however: the Earl's train was hauled by a former Midland Railway 0-6-0 tank engine, and not by the sole surviving 'J15', No. 65462, which is one of the North Norfolk's star attractions.* Although this locomotive is not known to have ever run on the Mid-Suffolk, it is identical to those John Hadfield observed in the line's last weeks of operation.

Passenger traffic during those final weeks was heavier than for years past - not that that was saying much - as people from near and far with fond if distant memories of the 'Middy' came to pay their last respects, locals who had always seen the line as an irrelevance finally roused themselves to sample its dubious

---

* One 'E4' ('Intermediate') as mentioned in the novel also survives: No. 62785 which has been exhibited at the National Railway Museum and more recently at Bressingham, near Diss. As has been mentioned, at least one locomotive of this class did run on the Mid-Suffolk.

The last train for Laxfield pulls in the crowds at Brockford; will a scene like this ever be repeated? *H.N. James*

The final train attracts local interest, and the odd captive spectator, as its four coaches block the level crossing at Laxfield. *H.N. James*

delights, and camera-wielding enthusiasts dashed off the trains at stopping places for an unrepeatable shot. On 12th July, with a fortnight to go, the BR Eastern Region Staff Railway Society paid a memorable farewell visit, taking the 11.15 am from Haughley and the 1.45 pm back from Laxfield. In the final week, to cope with the pressure, the line's two pairs of carriages ran coupled together. Children attending the Stowmarket schools gave No. 65447 a special send off as it pulled onto the branch for the last time with their train on the Friday afternoon, and the next day the community as a whole prepared to say its goodbyes.

Despite the sadness of the occasion, the Saturday dawned with a sense of anticipation among railway staff and 'civilians' alike. No. 65447 was polished until it shone for the last day of operation, and at 7.21 am it was ready to leave Laxfield with all four of the line's coaches. Driver Ernest Baker - stiff no doubt from his customary overnight 'kip' in the enginemen's mess - and fireman Ronald Thompson were on the footplate for the first round trip, after which they reported to Ipswich shed for further instructions. The first train of the day, which normally carried a mere handful of passengers, started with considerably more than that and others joined along the way; at Haughley a large number of day trippers were waiting to board, and throughout the day the numbers swelled, many taking the opportunity to visit a flower show and gymkhana at Laxfield.

Officially the very last train was the 3.55 pm from Haughley. The driver chosen for it was Joseph Skinner, later ironically a haulage contractor. His fireman, Jack Law, was by equal irony to finish his career as a 'top link' driver at Kings Cross, rostered regularly on the Leeds run. The guard we have met before: Willis Keeble, who as a schoolboy travelled on the very first train. He could not help contrasting the throng on that last Saturday in July with the virtually empty trains of previous months, remarking with an understandable touch of bitterness that 'there are always plenty of people who will go to a funeral'. Mr Keeble was to transfer to Ipswich, taking with him, as a link with the past, his MSLR guard's lamp.

There was one man aboard the train who had made even more journeys on the line than Mr Keeble: Mr Arthur Bowen of Laxfield, who had joined the Mid-Suffolk as a fireman in its very earliest years, graduating to driver and travelling the line an estimated 50,000 times before retiring in 1948. Mr Bowen brought with him, to the delight of railway 'brass' on the final trip, a model of one of the MSLR tank engines he had fired and driven before the LNER evicted them from the branch.

The platforms at Haughley were already packed and the temporary refreshment room organised by the station master overflowing as the final scheduled working from Laxfield pulled in, with its coaches already full and many passengers eager to join it for the return. Among the crowd was a party from County Hall, Ipswich, who had come in Edwardian dress as a reminder of the day in 1908 when the first passengers had travelled with such excitement. No. 65447 ran round its train and a wreath with abundant greenery was attached to the smokebox; more passengers climbed aboard and waited.

3.55 pm came and went and nothing happened. An announcement was made

Schoolchildren throng around No. 65467 at Laxfield when it took over their train shortly before closure. One lucky boy has made it to the footplate. *R.W. Kidner Collection*

that the locomotive of the connecting 1.30 from Liverpool Street had broken down, and that the Laxfield train would have to wait for it. Eventually the errant train limped in, and at 4.48 the 'right away' was given.

No. 65447 set off to attack Haughley Bank with an agility that defied both its 69 years and its heavy load, the never comfortable coaches being packed to the doors. As it forged on toward Laxfield, it steadily made up time in spite of photographic stops and other unscheduled halts, completing the journey in under 64 minutes. And as it rounded the final curve to arrive at Laxfield, there were cheers from a crowd of over a hundred who had gathered on the tiny platform.

That should have been the end of the story, but no-one seriously expected it to be. The train would normally have spent the weekend at Laxfield, but as there would be no Monday morning train and there were around 300 revellers waiting to return and only a few wagons ready to be cleared,* an extra train had been provided for. No. 65447 ran round its carriages for the last time, and the wreath was transferred to the rear of its tender. Railway officials climbed onto the footplate, and in a still packed carriage a passenger remarked: 'British Railways could make a profit if they announced that every train was a last one'. Then, amid a fusillade of detonators giving a haunting reminder of the first passenger train almost 44 years before, the very last one set off at 6.15 pm.

All along the line local people turned out even though the train was unscheduled, its progress being heralded with a hail of detonators. At Stradbroke the station master, Mr Edgar Gladwell, organist at Laxfield parish church, saw the train off for the last time before transferring to Framlingham for his final two years of service. With him were Mr Ollie Botwright, a clerk who was transferring to Ipswich after the best part of 30 years on the line, and Mr Harry Smith who, after 23 years as a porter, closed the level crossing gates for the last time. At Mendlesham a loudspeaker van played 'Land of Hope and Glory' and 'Auld Lang Syne', while waving his hat on the platform was the retired schoolmaster Mr Mayfield, who declared that 'as he had seen the first train come into Mendlesham, he would see the last one out'. No. 65447 continued to gain on conventional timings throughout its journey, but it was 7.20 pm before those waiting to greet it at Haughley station heard it coasting down the bank and watched as it took the connection to come to a halt with its train in the main line platform. The Mid-Suffolk Light Railway had carried its last public train, or so it seemed.

The engine shunted the four now surplus carriages into a siding, then ran on at 8.15 to Ipswich for allocation to other duties on the Monday. Driver Skinner and fireman Law reported to the shed, where their workmates were waiting to mark the occasion. Their final word to the reporter from the *Chronicle and Mercury* who had travelled with them for this poignant day was: 'Well, times change'.

---

* The story persists locally that either on this working or the final scheduled freight train the day before, an item of rolling stock was returned to the 'main line' which management had given up for lost years before.

The timber buildings of Laxfield station in a sorry state but still intact in June 1962, almost ten years after closure. The former headquarters of the line is in the foreground. *Author*

The only remaining part of the ex-GER station at Haughley in 1985. *Author*

Chapter Eight

Only a Memory

That was not quite the end of the original 'Middy'. There were materials to be recovered for which British Railways had further use despite the ramshackle and poverty stricken nature of the line, and still more than 30 wagons to be removed. No. 65388 returned on 6th August to clear the bulk of these, running up the branch tender first and having to be refilled with water from the pond on the Laxfield Mills branch because none was left in the tank by the engine shed. The locomotive marshalled the trucks on its way to Laxfield, began its return journey with seven open trucks plus a brake and reappeared at Haughley late in the day with an impressive array to take back to Ipswich.

The following day, 7th August, twelve days after the official 'last train', No. 65388 came back again, this time with a steam crane from Colchester to remove the now empty main water tank from Laxfield, ultimately for use on the Festiniog Railway which in 1952 appeared even more of a lost cause than the Mid-Suffolk. The train left Haughley at 8.45 am and spent all day on the branch; the locomotive's water ran low and, with none on tap at Laxfield, the fireman again had to refill the boiler by bucket from the pond. As all telephones had also been removed after closure, there was no way of reporting progress to the world outside, and the signalman at Haughley must have been wondering what had happened to the train when it loomed out of the darkness at 8.30 that night. No. 65388 made at least one more trip down the branch, running boiler first; it was last observed at Laxfield Mills in June 1953, an eyewitness describing it as 'rusting and on its last legs'.

By now, a contractor - Connell's of Coatbridge - had been appointed to lift the track of the entire line apart from a headshunt to be left at Haughley. A four-wheel diesel shunter and a crane were delivered by road to Laxfield on 1st August, 1953 and work commenced . . . only to be interrupted when the crane proved too heavy for the original MSLR track at Laxfield Mills. Nevertheless the half-mile of track beyond Laxfield station had gone by 30th August when No. 65404, making as far as is known the final steam-hauled passage of the entire 'Middy', brought a train of empty wagons to Laxfield which on the return run were loaded with reusable materials already set aside by the contractor. The county Highways Department had by now tarred over the level crossing at Wilby, but No. 65404 dealt with the usurpation of the motor age by simply gouging its way through.

From then onward, Nos. 65388 and 65404 made regular forays up the branch - initially to Kenton and by early 1954 over a steadily shorter distance - to haul stored wagonloads of track panels back to Haughley. On 25th April, 1954 the task was completed with the installation of a buffer stop at the end of the Haughley headshunt, which still passed over Haugh Lane bridge to terminate where the signal protecting the station approach had until recently stood. That such trouble was gone to was ironic given that from the removal of the Cratfield extension in 1916 until the lifting of the track at Laxfield Mills, the end of the

'Middy' had been marked only by a pile of rotting sleepers. More ironic still, those buffers and the line up to them lasted only a decade.

The only place where trains continued to be seen was Haughley, where the junction between the two main lines continued in being, virtually unaffected by the closure. Forms of traction changed from steam to diesel, but trains from Ipswich to Norwich, Cambridge and the Midlands continued to pass through or stop, and the mail trains to cross and connect in the small hours. The first sign of change was the disappearance of exchange traffic between the Bury and Norwich lines. Then, in 1960, the bay platform where Mid-Suffolk trains had terminated was removed, and finally, in 1964, the Pure Seed Co. went over entirely to road traffic. Haughley yard formally closed at the end of that year, and in due course the headshunt - the final stretch of Mid-Suffolk track - was lifted.

By now Haughley's future as a passenger station was also under threat. The local passenger trains - nine a day to Bury and four to Norwich - which had increasingly become the reason for so small a village retaining its station were ever more lightly used. Of the other stations between Ipswich and Norwich, first Bramford and then Claydon closed, then in 1964 closure notices were posted for Haughley itself, along with all other stations between Cambridge, Ely, Norwich and Ipswich except for Diss, Bury, Newmarket and Stowmarket. The closure processes took time to operate in the face of strong objections, with Dullingham, Kennett, Thurston and Elmswell between Cambridge and Haughley all being reprieved for 'paytrain' operation. But in mid-1966 Ministerial sanction was given for the closure of the remaining stations* including Haughley. The station was given a further lease of life when a dispute between British Rail and the National Union of Railwaymen held up implementation, but once this was resolved its fate was sealed. Haughley station closed with effect from 2nd January, 1967, and the final operating link with the Mid-Suffolk Light Railway had gone.

Haughley remained the divergence of two reasonably important lines, with container traffic for Felixstowe Docks superseding much of the general freight, but one more fundamental change lay ahead: the electrification of the Norwich line, which was to transform the face of Haughley Junction in 1984-85. Almost all surviving station buildings were removed and redundant trackwork lifted including the last of the sidings; a high speed crossover was laid where the station had been and the turnout to the Bury line singled, though the route became double immediately after. An automatic level crossing with a well-displayed warning to drivers of tall vehicles of the perils of 25 kv overhead wires was installed. There were few reminders left of the station as it had been apart from a small part of the station building beside the crossing lettered 'Haughley Junction', and siding spaces beside and beyond the silo where trains to Laxfield had begun their attack on Haughley Bank. Haugh Lane bridge remained, but its deck had long since gone.

Along the route of the Mid-Suffolk, long stretches of trackbed returned speedily to the plough, a process assisted by the general lack of earthworks; the most obvious piece of civil engineering, the cutting east of Mendlesham and the bridge carrying the A140 over it, disappeared when the road was upgraded in 1968. By 1970 the line could be singled out by the Countryside Commission as

---

* Needham Market was among those initially closed, but reopened not long after.

having presented fewer obstacles to reversion to agricultural use than almost
any other in the country. The station buildings proved rather more durable,
possibly because of their inconvenient locations; those at Laxfield and
Stradbroke remained intact on site well into the 1970s and at Mendlesham they
also survived for a considerable time. In his *Shell Guide to Suffolk* Norman Scarfe
wrote of the scene two decades after closure:

> Pathetic little corrugated-iron pavilions that were erected at stations on the Mid-Suffolk
> Light Railway stand as derelict memorials to that belated attempt to supply good
> transport facilities to the country people of central Suffolk.

At Kenton, a carriage believed to have been one of the MSLR's original stock
outlived the station buildings, being used minus its chassis as a store, but by the
1970s it too had gone. It was to be 1987 before the last MSLR station building
in situ, at Horham, was removed . . . fortunately for re-use as a station!

Many locals must have taken stock on the day of closure and since, and
wondered if the brief life of the Mid-Suffolk Light Railway was worth the
candle. On the one hand, its promoters suffered huge personal losses, on the
other, it brought very real benefits to an isolated part of the country for almost
half a century. Had the Westerfield section been built, maybe the system or part
of it would have survived into East Anglia's current era of prosperity. But as
operated, the line was probably fated from the start to a lingering decline. The
Eastern Counties bus services which competed with and supplanted it have
fared little better; by the time deregulation came in the 1980s, Laxfield was
down to just one bus a day, running between Stradbroke and Saxmundham.
Debenham has kept a better bus service, with various independently-operated
routes to Ipswich, showing once again where the traffic potential has always
been. As for the railways, they were to retreat throughout the area until only
the Bury, Norwich and East Suffolk lines and the Felixstowe branch could boast
a passenger service, plus occasional freight trains as far as Leiston on the
Aldeburgh branch to collect nuclear flasks from Sizewell.

By the close of the 1980s the Mid-Suffolk Light Railway was an increasingly
distant memory to the inhabitants of the area it had served, with a small number
of relics surviving as much through chance and nostalgia on the part of the
families of former employees as through any co-ordinated effort to preserve them.
One of the MSLR's trademarks was the style of its station nameboards and speed
restriction signs: grey and white with a unique, almost *art nouveau*, type of
lettering. The nameboards from Kenton station were displayed at the original
Museum of British Transport at Clapham and are now in store at the National
Railway Museum in York; the MSLR Society has requested that one be loaned for
display at Brockford. Those from Wilby were also rescued, by an exile from the
area, Mr Reginald Jennings of Salisbury. Of larger items which survived for a
while, the water tank that found its way to the Festiniog Railway was not of
interest in its own right, and the ex-M&GN water carrier so nearly saved in 1970
would mainly have been of interest to devotees of East Anglia's largest
independent line. It was, incidentally, the M&GN Preservation Society, now the
North Norfolk Railway, which preserved the last 'J15'; it would have been a

tragedy if none of this large, versatile and long-lived class had been saved and there would have been wide appreciation had more than one survived. Incidentally, No. 65462 was not the M&GNRS's original choice; No. 65469 was first selected from the scrap road at Stratford, but turned out to have a cracked frame.

There has also been keen interest in Mid-Suffolk tickets, reflected in the price paid when one came up at auction at Phillips in October 1985. A lot comprising an early MSLR single ticket from Laxfield to Wilby and a ticket from the Colne Valley and Halstead Railway in Essex was knocked down for £100, well in excess of the price predicted. If anyone had told the original purchaser of that ticket in the line's earliest days that it would one day be resold for £50 or so, his or her reaction would have been one of incredulity. Salerooms apart, one other early MSLR ticket found its way into the small exhibits section of the National Railway Museum.

The course of the line was largely eradicated, though some sections of trackbed survived as farm tracks and occasionally a sudden hump in a country lane bespoke the sight of a level crossing. The embankments between Gipping and Mendlesham, Horham and Stradbroke and Kenton and Debenham survived, as did the brickwork though not the deck of the Aspall Road bridge. Most station sites became agricultural or council depots with no clue as to their previous purpose beyond, sometimes, a short brick platform or, as at Laxfield, three submerged by undergrowth. The memory of the line was preserved in 'Old Station Road' at Mendlesham and - for a time - in 'Old Station Yard', the title bestowed on the station site at Brockford by the firm who occupied it.

Passengers flashing by the patch of bushes and cinders marking the Mid-Suffolk junction at Haughley became increasingly hard put from their air-conditioned electric-hauled comfort to imagine what it was like to travel in those elderly mixed trains to Laxfield. It is even harder, standing on the platform at Aspall next to a heap of sugar beet awaiting shipment by road, to imagine that rose-framed nameboards once told the passenger he was miles from anywhere. The Mid-Suffolk Light Railway deserved a better epitaph than that, but for more than three decades after closure seemed fated not to have it.

Horham station still *in situ* in 1985, more than three decades after the last passengers used it. Three years later it was to be saved for preservation.   *Author*

Chapter Nine

A New Beginning

Despite its near-eradication by the end of the 1980s, the Mid-Suffolk Light Railway was destined to be more than a fast-receding chapter in history, being eventually re-created on a much more modest scale through the agency of devoted railway preservationists.

The reincarnation first took visible form not in Suffolk but at Mangapps Farm outside Burnham-on-Crouch in Essex, where a railway museum opened amid 430 acres of crops in August 1989 thanks to the enterprise of the farmer, Mr John Jolly, and his wife. Pride of place among the first major exhibits went to the Horham station building, which was brought to the site in 1988 after other efforts to preserve it proved abortive and restored to serve as terminus of a short length of working railway. Despite 35 years of disuse, the only parts that had to be replaced were the corrugated iron roof sheets, the barge boards, some floorboards and the door of the booking office . . . replaced with the door from Trowse Swing Bridge Junction signal box, Norwich. The Horham building shares the terminal platform with a smaller shelter retrieved from Brampton, on the East Suffolk line, but probably of M&GN origin. It is eerie to anyone who saw Horham station so recently marooned on its original platform to buy a ticket at the booking office window and stand under its GER brown-and-cream painted shelter waiting for a train, amid busier scenes than it had ever witnessed on its home turf. Even better was to come, however. In May 1993 Maldon District Council gave planning permission for an extension of the running line to two-thirds of a mile . . . with the terminal at the far end to be the former Laxfield station building, which after removal from its original site served for a time as a sports pavilion at Bedfield before being rescued for preservation. Among a splendid collection of smaller relics, Mangapps can also boast an MSLR train staff.

Ironically it was the survival of the Laxfield building in brief exile at Bedfield that spurred the rebirth of the 'Middy'. Paul Davey, founder of the MSLR Society, says that the sight of it there in 1988

. . . prompted me to wonder whether it could be preserved in a railway setting as the focal point of a small MSLR museum. It was important to me that museum should be in Suffolk, preferably near to the original railway. I was confident that such a scheme could succeed because it would be on a modest scale and the principal exhibit was relatively easy to move. I drafted a proposal and forwarded it to the Museum of East Anglian Life in Stowmarket. They gave the proposal serious consideration but decided that it would be beyond them financially.

At that point in early 1990 I could have given up. For some reason, however, I decided that a way must be found. I was grateful for the support of my friends in Stowmarket Railway Club who probably thought I was mad but never said so! Those friends (in particular David Chappell and Bob Boardman) were to become more involved as the year went on.

I began to look at Mid-Suffolk station sites to see whether any of them had potential as an MSLR museum. Brockford seemed to offer the most potential. There were no near

Horham station building in service again, as a terminus of the working railway at Mangapps Farm museum near Burnham-on-Crouch. Approaching is a train headed by *Demelza*, a Bagnall 0-6-0 saddle tank built in 1954. The signal cabin is from Berney Arms and the platform seat from the London, Tilbury & Southend Railway.

Colloryan

The 'Middy' open for visitors: Brockford station sets out its wares in May 1995. The crossing gate is some 50 yards short of the road, where the line originally crossed *en route* for Mendlesham.

David Chappell

neighbours to object, it is the easiest site to reach from a main road, and of course the cattle dock survived.

I wrote to the landowner, Mr Tony Alston, to enquire whether he would be prepared to lease an area of land for the establishment of a small museum. Imagine my surprise and delight when he responded favourably to the idea! On a Monday evening at the end of August 1990 my friends and I had our first meeting at Brockford with Tony Alston. He was prepared not only to lease us the museum site at a peppercorn rent, but also make available two-thirds of a mile of trackbed in the Aspall direction that he also owned.

On 28th November, 1990, 70 local people and enthusiasts met at the district council social club in Needham Market to form the Mid-Suffolk Light Railway Society. By the autumn of 1994 it would have 149 members, 70 per cent of them living in Suffolk, with supporters raising £1,000 toward the project in just six months. At the inaugural meeting Mr Davey was elected chairman of the embryo society; he told the *East Anglian Daily Times*:

> The original 60 ft cattle dock is still at Brockford, and that will be extended by 70 ft to the length of a platform on the Mid-Suffolk Light Railway. We aim to erect an appropriate building on the platform and build a typical Mid-Suffolk Light Railway track layout more than half a mile in length on the route of the original trackbed.

The formal aims of the Society are as follows:

1. The setting up of a working Museum dedicated to the re-creation of a typical Mid-Suffolk Light Railway station and environs, complete with appropriate rolling stock and motive power.
2. The ultimate restoration of part of the original route of the Railway to become a working railway.
3. The preservation of artefacts, memorabilia, recollections and reminiscences of the Railway.
4. The stimulation of educational and historical interest in the Railway.
5. The securement of a long term future for the Museum for future generations.

Work at Brockford began in January 1991, and the following year temporary planning permission for the museum and a short length of track was granted.

Crucial to the success of the scheme was the enthusiasm of Mr Alston, who was elected the Society's first president; quite apart from making most of the Brockford station site available, he has on numerous occasions lent tractors and other equipment to bring materials to the museum. In 1996 he lent the Society the middle unit of his industrial buildings for carriage and wagon restoration. The Society's prospects were further enhanced when Mid-Suffolk District Council, successor of Hartismere council which petitioned against the closure, threw its weight behind the scheme with financial backing as well as planning permission.

Just how quickly the dream of a meticulously restored Mid-Suffolk station came to fruition was demonstrated in 1994 when the Association of Railway Preservation Societies gave Brockford the *Railway World* commendation in its Best Restored Railway Station competition, the judges particularly noting the tidiness of the site, not a common feature of preserved railways. The former cattle dock was indeed rebuilt as a full passenger platform, being raised in the

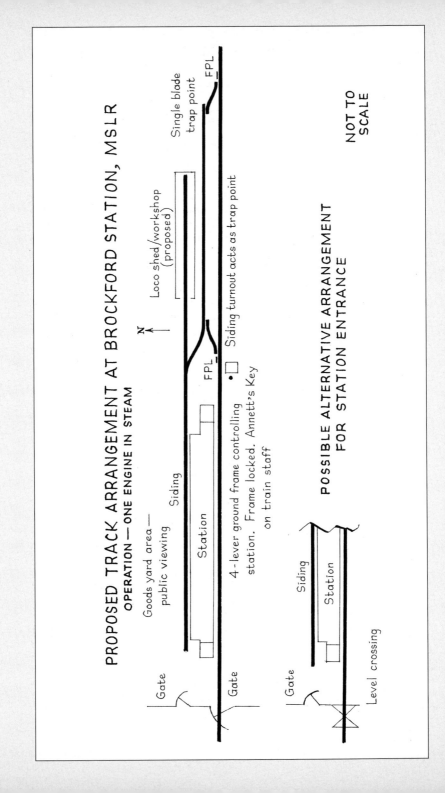

PROPOSED TRACK ARRANGEMENT AT BROCKFORD STATION, MSLR
OPERATION—ONE ENGINE IN STEAM

Goods yard area—
public viewing

Siding

Station

Gate

Gate

Gate

N

Loco shed/workshop
(proposed)

Single blade
trap point

FPL

FPL

4-lever ground frame controlling
station. Frame locked. Annett's Key
on train staff

■ ● Siding turnout acts as trap point

POSSIBLE ALTERNATIVE ARRANGEMENT
FOR STATION ENTRANCE

Gate

Siding

Station

Level crossing

NOT TO
SCALE

process, and on it were installed original MSLR buildings from Mendlesham, Wilby and Brockford itself, all carefully restored, to re-create a typical scene from the line's independent existence. Of these the Mendlesham building, ceremonially re-opened on 18th July, 1993 and housing a GER table, chair and ticket rack and a Mid-Suffolk inkwell, was the most remarkable survival, having been dismantled in 1953 and reassembled for use as a hen house at Old Newton. It was removed from there, section by section, in 1992 and painstakingly restored at Brockford, in the process gaining the original booking office door from Kenton. Also in the society's possession, but safely in store, is the original station building from Cratfield, which had miraculously survived for 80 years since its brief use for a railway purpose, and a GER workshop and shed from Mellis. Among smaller items at Brockford is the original MSLR station lamp from Aspall; maybe it will one day 'go home'. The platform also boasts a rose grown from a cutting taken by the widow of Walter Flatman, porter at Wilby for twenty years, from the plant he tended at the line's smallest station.

Brockford station, open on Sundays, Bank Holidays and some Wednesdays from Easter to the end of September, has played host to a wide range of special events including Great Eastern days, Edwardian days and commemorations of anniversaries in the life of the 'Middy', such as the 90th anniversary in 1994 of the opening of the line to freight traffic; the aim of these is both to raise funds and to raise the profile of the railway locally as work continued. For Mr Davey - who stood down as Chairman in November 1993, David Chappell replacing him after retiring early from ICI to spend more time on the railway - the most poignant was the commemoration of the 40th anniversary of closure, in July 1992, with everyone who had travelled on the last train invited for a reunion. 'It was a wonderful day', he recalls.

The weather was kind, the Suffolk Concert Band played and there was a wonderful turnout by 'last dayers'. It was a truly memorable day with a great atmosphere, and convinced us that the creation of the museum was important not only in railway terms but also for its part in the history of the area.

In September 1994 a Railway Letter Service, using special Mid-Suffolk stamps, was begun as a fund-raising venture. A footpath has been set out on the first mile of trackbed toward Aspall, with surviving Mid-Suffolk fencing, gateposts and even signs visible; a pond just beyond the station rapidly became a favourite picnic spot for visitors. Paying visitors in 1995 neared the 2,000 mark, well up on the year before but still short of the 5,000 needed before a brown sign directing tourists to the line could be erected on the A140, a mile and a half away.

It was the prospect of an influx of traffic from the main road along narrow country lanes which led the Mid-Suffolk Council Planning Committee to turn down in late 1996 an application to extend the museum and construct a running line. As this book went to press, efforts were under way to resolve this impasse with a more modest application.

Links with the past, and hopes of a steam-hauled service on the 'Middy' once again, were strengthened by the acquisition of a Hudswell, Clarke 0-6-0 saddle tank, maker's number 1604, from the former Lincolnshire Railway Museum at

Burgh-le-Marsh. Built in 1928 for the Lincolnshire Beet Sugar Company who numbered it '1', it worked for 45 years at the company's Bardney plant before being presented to the Nene Valley Railway, whence it passed to the Lincolnshire museum, initially at Kirton Lindsey. The Mid-Suffolk society obtained it on a five-year loan from the NVR when the Burgh-le-Marsh museum site closed in 1994, bringing it to Brockford the following year. While much more recent than the MSLR's three locomotives from the same manufacturer and clearly of industrial design, it was a highly appropriate acquisition; it is, however, a static exhibit and major works would be required to get it back in steam. In the interim, agreement was reached in principle in 1996 to take an 0-6-0 diesel-mechanical shunter from one of the unsuccessful bidders in the contest to preserve the Epping-Ongar branch.

Three former Great Eastern coaches have been slated for restoration. No. 1266, a five-compartment third class carriage brought from Henley near Ipswich in 1991 and mounted on LMS tube wagon wheelframes obtained from Chesterfield, is being steadily restored by a team led by Paul Davey, now a vice-president of the society as is Peter Paye, whose book is the preservationists' 'Bible'. Materials - notably brass door handles and hinges - from the body of GER four-compartment luggage composite No. 205, which was past saving when located in an orchard near Bury St Edmunds, have been incorporated; spares have also been offered from GER No. 200, vandalised during rebuilding on the North Downs Steam Railway in Kent.

The second Great Eastern coach intended for use on the line is No. 13, a two-compartment brake third owned by the society and being restored at Brockford by a group of members; the underframe from a BR standard 20-ton brake van on site will be used once it has been shortened by the necessary 16 inches.

The third Great Eastern carriage, three-compartment first No. 140 dating from the 1860s, is also being restored privately by a group of Society members at a farm near Stowmarket, having been retrieved in 1995 from a garden at Elmswell.

Restoration of No. 131, a North Eastern Railway passenger-rated van for the carriage of milk, parcels and perishables, is an even bigger task. Society member Graham Ashwell found the carriage on a British Rail site at Ipswich and bought it for £45 from a scrap dealer. Three further GER coach bodies arrived in September 1996, one having been lived in as a bungalow just ten days before. All three date from 1876; two are 5-compartment, the other a 4-wheeled full brake. One is being pressed into use as a refreshment coach for the 1997 season to free up No. 1266 for full restoration.

A number of goods wagons complete the tally of rolling stock. A Great Eastern open wagon was donated in 1994 by David Rouse of Williton, Somerset and brought from the West Somerset Railway after being damaged there in a shunting accident. LNER Toad B goods brake van No. 157787, identical to those used on the Mid-Suffolk in latter years, was delivered in the autumn of 1994, sadly after having been burnt by vandals at Tunbridge Wells. Bodywork from the BR standard brake is being used to repair it. Also undergoing restoration are BR open wagon No. 492135, in the guise of a Moy coal wagon as seen on the line, three GER box vans (one the first to arrive on site in 1993 after being spotted at Cantley, near Norwich, and two from the North Norfolk Railway where they held parts for the last surviving 'J15'), and LMS horse box No. 42598, built at Derby in 1948/49. Also on site is a rather strange flat wagon from the North Downs Railway, formerly used for carrying pallets of cement, not the least of its peculiarities is that it is unbraked.

Most hopefully, trackwork - some of it flat-bottom and fixed in the MSLR manner - has been laid in the station area, starting by the platform near the replica level crossing and heading toward Aspall as far as finances, planning permission and the availability of the former trackbed permit. Eighty yards of running line were purchased from a member of the Nene Valley Railway in 1994, and other track and pointwork has come from a Co-op site at Derby Road, Ipswich and from the Spa Valley Railway at Tunbridge Wells. The layout has been designed by society Secretary Rob Murray to meet five aims: to fit the restricted site, use the materials the society owned, facilitate operation as a working terminus with one locomotive, resemble an MSLR station layout, and satisfy the Railway Inspectorate.

On 24th November, 1994, the society concluded a 21-year lease from Mr Alston at a peppercorn rent of the station site, 1,200 yards of trackbed and enough land at the Aspall end of it for a second station with siding and loop. In preparation for a working railway, a new Mid-Suffolk Light Railway Company was born, with Paul Jeffery taking over the chair from David Chappell, to take the place of the society. Its immediate aim was 'Project 98' - for the construction and operation of a 400 yard stretch of track to 'Blacksmith's Green', from September 1998, using coaches No. 1266 and either the Toad brake van or coach No. 13, with either the diesel or a hired-in steam locomotive.

These ambitions were put on hold by the refusal of planning permission, but hopes remained undimmed.

That is where matters stood at the time of writing. From being a fading memory, the 'Middy' has been brought back to life as, initially, the only standard gauge railway museum in Suffolk, and the rebirth of the line itself has become more than an improbable dream. If the hard work and commitment of the leading lights in the Mid-Suffolk society are properly rewarded, we may one day see steam trains running once again between Brockford and Aspall . . . and maybe even further. At long last one of England's most colourful railways is getting not simply a second life, but the recognition it seemed fated never to enjoy.

The track layout at Brockford, seen from the running line in the direction of Aspall. Two of the carriage bodies for restoration can just be seen on the right.   *David Chappell*

Sources

Official records apart, a number of books and magazine and newspaper articles have been of considerable help in the compilation and updating of this book. Most heavily relied on has been Peter Paye's authoritative book *The Mid-Suffolk Light Railway*, published by Wild Swan in 1986. This comprehensive work, running to 216 pages, not only gives a wealth of valuable detail but tells the story of the 'Middy' with grace and affection. For the story of the rebirth of the line at Brockford as well as reminiscences of the past, I have been almost as dependent on *Making Tracks*, the quarterly journal of the Mid-Suffolk Light Railway Society.

I have also made considerable use of the following:

Books
East Anglian Branch Line Album, Dr I.C. Allen, Oxford Publishing Co., 1977.
Love On A Branch Line, John Hadfield, Hutchinson, 1959; Alastair Press: hardback 1988, paperback 1995.
Steam In The Blood, R.H.N. Hardy, Ian Allan, 1971.
Ipswich and District Transport Historical Society Handbook, 1967/68.

Magazines:
The Locomotive, May 1907, pp. 84-6.
Railway Magazine, July-December 1924, pp. 347-52.
Railway World, October-November 1952, pp. 232-4, 283/4.
Trains Illustrated, October 1952, pp. 373-7.

Newspapers:
East Anglian Daily Times, 30th September, 1908.
Chronicle and Mercury, 1st August, 1952.

Numerous shorter references to various aspects of the line can be found in:

British Railways and the Great War, pp. 54/5, 423.
Britain's Railway Liveries, E.F. Carter (3rd edition, 1963).
Disused Railways of England and Wales, Countryside Commission, 1970.
Standard Gauge Light Railways, R.W. Kidner, Oakwood Press, 1954.
The Light Railway Handbook, R.W. Kidner, Oakwood Press, 1962.
0-6-0 Tanks of the GER, P. Proud, Railway Correspondence and Travel Society, 1954.
Trains Annual, 1952, Ian Allan.
Branch Line Album, P.B. Whitehouse, Ian Allan, 1962.
Minor Railways of England and their Locomotives, George Woodcock, Goose & Son, 1970.

Magazine articles:
Eastern Region Magazine, November 1952.
The Locomotive, 15th October, 1904; 15th October, 1908; 15th January, 1909.
Railway Magazine: November 1923; March and June 1937; November 1939; September 1952; October 1957; August 1961; December 1962; July 1990; January and May 1993; May, August, September and October 1994.
Railways: July 1952.
Railway Observer: 1952 (p.109).
Railway World: May 1994.